# Shape it & Bake it

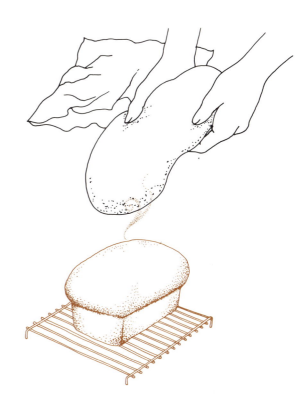

Quick and Simple Ideas
For Children
From Frozen Bread Dough

### by Sylvia Ogren

DILLON PRESS, INC./Minneapolis, Minnesota 55415

©1981 by Dillon Press, Inc. All rights reserved

Dillon Press, Inc., 500 South Third Street
Minneapolis, Minnesota 55415

Printed in the United States of America

Library of Congress Cataloging in Publication Data

Ogren, Sylvia.

    Shape it and bake it.

    (Doing and learning books)
    Includes index.
    SUMMARY: Helpful hints and drawings accompany step-by-step directions for making a variety of breads, dinner rolls, sweet rolls, coffee cakes, ethnic breads, and supper and snack breads from frozen dough.
    I. Bread—Juvenile literature. [I. Bread] I. Title. II. Series.
TX769.038                  641.8'15                  79-23923
ISBN 0-87518-193-7

*Cover photo courtesy Rhodes Frozen Bread Dough*

# Contents

Introduction .................................. 5

The Story of Bread........................... 7

Special Know-How for Baking
   with Frozen Dough ....................... 11

Bread Loaves ................................ 15

Dinner Rolls ................................. 33

Sweet Rolls .................................. 47

Coffee Cakes................................. 61

Ethnic Breads ............................... 79

Supper and Snack Breads .................... 87

Special Recipes.............................. 102

    Icings

    Egg Wash

    Cinnamon-Sugar

    Sugar

    Streusel

Index........................................ 104

# Introduction

One of my secret desires as a youngster was to bake bread that was as good as my mother's. One day, when my parents were on vacation, I decided this was my time to bake bread. I found a recipe, described step-by-step in photos, and I followed it exactly, or so I thought. My very first dinner rolls looked beautiful, but they had one problem—they were so salty we really didn't enjoy eating them. Knowing today that the amount of salt controls the rising, I have often wondered why the rolls rose so nicely!

Today many people are once more baking bread at home. Frozen bread dough is one of the reasons for the change. Why? Frozen bread dough has made it possible for everyone—yes, everyone—to bake bread. The dough is already made for you. And yet you can have the fun that comes from shaping the dough, watching it rise, and then, smelling the aroma of fresh-baked bread and finally tasting something you have made yourself that is done just right. You can't add too much salt! Place a loaf of frozen dough in the refrigerator in the morning before you go to school, and it will be thawed when you come home.

One of my purposes in writing this cookbook is to share with you some of the fun that I have had baking bread. As you look through the book, you will find easy, mouth-watering recipes to try. Before you do any baking, read "Special Know-How for Baking with Frozen Bread," page

11, as well as the tips at the beginning of each section. There you will find important information that you need to know about bread baking. It will contribute to your success.

Now, you are ready for a new hobby. Bread baking.

Bake bread for the family.

Bake bread for special gifts.

Bake bread for your parties.

Once you have tasted home-baked bread, you will want to continue baking it. Perhaps you will become the regular bread baker in your family.

Happy Baking!

# The Story of Bread

The story of bread is old, so old that it began before history was written down. Indeed, bread is thought to have been the first human food. A type of flour was made by crushing wild grain seeds between flat stones. These crushed seeds were found to taste better when combined with water and then baked on hot rocks in the sun. It was a flat, unleavened bread very different from anything we eat today. With the passage of time people learned which grains made the best bread. Eventually wheat was grown to make bread. The growing of grains, including wheat, had its beginning in the fertile river valleys of the Middle East.

Crude ovens have been found that were in use four thousand years ago. About 600 B.C. the first "beehive" shaped ovens were made. These ovens were a great improvement over earlier ones. They were closed on the top so the bread would brown better. Eventually the oven was surrounded with brick to help keep the heat in for better baking and browning. A chimney was added for the smoke to escape. (Hearths similar to the beehive ovens are still used for baking breads in some countries.) Long-handled wooden paddles were used to slip the bread into the oven. When the bread was baked, these same paddles removed it from the oven. Perhaps you have seen these wooden paddles used in a pizza shop.

For hundreds of years, bread was flat. Then the first raised bread was made, perhaps by accident. No one really knows exactly how it happened. All accounts agree, however, that it happened in Egypt sometime between 1450 B.C. and 3000 B.C. Someone—a slave, a homemaker, or a baker—set the dough in the sun and forgot it for a long time, perhaps a couple of days. When he or she returned to the dough, it had risen. Curious to see what had happened to the dough, the Egyptian baked it and tasted it. This was the beginning of raised bread. From Egypt the making of raised breads spread to Greece, then to Rome, and from there through Northern Europe.

It was not until the seventeenth century that scientists first saw yeast under the microscope and learned how it caused bread dough to rise. Spores of this tiny one-celled plant were carried in the air. Given enough time, the yeast would grow in the warm dough. As the plants grew, they gave off a gas in a process called fermentation. The bread dough was elastic enough to trap this gas, and the dough rose. When the bread was baked, the yeast was killed, and the bread held its risen shape. Until yeast was made commercially, the process of making raised bread was slow. Doughs would be set in a warm place to ferment and rise. When it was discovered that some of the dough could be saved and added to the new dough, it hastened the process. Eventually sour dough and potato water starters were developed. With starters, the dough had to be prepared the night before, and many times baking was not completed until late the next day. It was not until yeast was widely sold in stores in the early 1900s that bread could be made and baked in a few hours at home.

In the late 1930s and early 1940s, it was noted that certain diseases caused by a lack of the B vitamins could be prevented by putting the vitamins back into the flour or bread. The first enrichment laws were passed in 1941. Many bakers and millers agreed to enrich their bread and flour. Today most states have enrichment laws, and most of the bread and flour sold is enriched. Be sure the white bread or flour you buy has been enriched.

Enriched breads and cereals are important sources of three B vitamins—riboflavin, niacin, and thiamine. They also provide us with carbohydrates, starches, and sugars, which give us the quick energy necessary to start the day. A sandwich with a glass of milk is an excellent, inexpensive source of good protein. This is why breads and cereals make up one of the four basic food groups necessary for good nutrition. Four or more servings daily is recommended. Because of the extra energy they use, young people should eat six or seven servings daily.

Except for the Far East, where rice is the mainstay of the diet, bread is still the universal food around the world. Just what kind of bread people like to eat depends on what ingredients have been available to them. For example, there are different leavening, or rising, agents. Not all breads are yeast leavened. Some have baking powder or baking soda leavening. Breads like matzoth and tortillas have no leavening at all. In the section of this book called "Ethnic Breads," you will find recipes for breads from other countries that you can bake in your own kitchen.

The story of bread would make an interesting paper for a school class. Choose breads as your topic and then do some more reading in reference books. For a hobby and some fun in the kitchen, choose bread baking and start with the frozen dough—today's easiest and most foolproof method for home-baked bread.

# Special Know-How for Baking with Frozen Dough

## Thawing Frozen Dough

Place a loaf of frozen dough in a large plastic bag or in a well-greased pan and cover it loosely.

* Dough can be thawed at room temperature. It will take several hours. In the refrigerator, it will thaw overnight.

* If you want to thaw the dough more quickly, choose one of the following places:
    In front of a sunny window
    Near a steady flow of warm air
    On top of a range warmed by a pilot light

* If you have an electric oven, here is a good thawing and rising method to use. Place a pan of boiling water on the bottom shelf. Set the pan of bread dough on the shelf above the water. (Do not turn on oven heat.) Reheat water one or two times while bread is rising. Do not cover the bread dough, because the steam keeps it moist. Ten minutes before baking, take out the risen bread and preheat the oven. This method takes four to five hours. If this method is used in an oven with a pilot light, keep the oven door open about two inches.

* Here's another fast way to let dough thaw and rise. Heat the oven to 200° F. Then turn off the heat (this is very important) and put the frozen dough in the oven. Place a pan of boiling water in the oven to keep the top moist. With a gas oven, keep the door ajar about two inches so the bread won't get too warm from the pilot light.

## Thawing Frozen Dough in the Microwave Oven

The fastest method for thawing frozen dough is in the microwave oven. It is very important that you understand the power levels of the microwave oven, because it is easy to overheat the dough and kill the yeast. If the yeast is killed, the dough will not rise. Have an adult help you the first time you thaw the dough in the microwave oven.

* Place 1 to 1½ cups hot water in a flat dish larger than your bread loaf pan. *Be sure to use only glass or microwave-proof dishes or pans.* Grease the bread pan heavily, and butter the frozen loaf of dough on all sides. Put the loaf in the bread pan and set in the dish of water in the microwave oven. Cover with waxed paper.

* Microwave at half power (50 percent, medium, or defrost for most ovens) 4 minutes. Turn the dish holding the water ¼ turn every minute. Then let it stand in the oven 10 minutes. Continue the process—microwaving for 1 minute and resting for 10 minutes—until the dough is thawed and slightly warm. Rotate ¼ turn after each rest period.

* If the oven has 30 percent power, microwave 6 minutes, turning every 1½ minutes. With 10 percent power, microwave 15 minutes, turning every 5 minutes.

* After thawing, reshape the dough into a loaf as described for An Old-Fashioned Loaf, page 22, or cover and let rise until doubled in size. Then shape, let rise, and bake as directed in recipe.

## Use Good Baking Techniques

To make a basic loaf of bread, follow the directions on the label. For delicious variations, use one of the recipes in this book. No matter how you use your bread dough, you should read the tips and suggestions that follow.

* Read the recipe before you start baking. Be sure you have all the ingredients.

* Use a soft brush for spreading butter or egg white on bread dough. (A good one is a soft paint brush about one inch wide.) A soft brush is especially important if the shaped dough has risen before it is brushed.

* Cover bread loosely with plastic wrap or slip it into a large plastic bag when it is rising, unless the recipe says otherwise. Dust the plastic wrap lightly with flour. It will help to keep it from sticking to the dough. Be sure to allow space for the bread to rise. Making a tent cover with aluminum foil works well, too. If the bread is not covered, it can form a crust on top and not rise well.

* *Temperature* is very important in determining how long it will take for the dough to rise. With frozen dough you can control the time needed for rising by controlling the temperature. Then you can have the bread ready at the time you want to bake it. If the temperature is about 90° F., a loaf can thaw and rise and be ready to bake in four hours or less. At a temperature of 70° F., you can expect the bread to take at least six hours to rise.

* About ten minutes before the bread is ready to bake, preheat the oven to the temperature given in the recipe. Then it will be at the right temperature when you are ready to put the bread in the oven.

## Rolling Out Frozen Dough for Recipes

Bread dough is elastic and springy. The dough will spring back when rolling it out for cinnamon rolls, coffee cakes, and other products. To make it easier to roll out, let the dough rise until doubled in size. Place the dough on a lightly floured surface, handling it as little as possible. If you don't have a large breadboard for rolling out the dough, use the countertop surface. Do not use a pastry cloth for bread dough.

  Do not knead or reshape the dough into a ball. Reshaping makes it hard to roll out. Start rolling and stretching the dough to the size you need. Lift the dough up and reflour the surface lightly if necessary. You may want to turn the dough over. Don't flour too heavily. Let the dough stick to the board a few places along the edges.

# Bread Loaves

A loaf of bread is the easiest place for the first-time baker to start. In this section you'll find round loaves, flat loaves, long loaves, squatty loaves, and high, light loaves. You'll find loaves embraced with a butter-rich crust or snuggled under a crackling toasty coating. Your bread can look like bread baked on a hearth or in Grandma's wood range. Grandma spent hours making the bread that you can bake with very little effort!

To start, look at the recipes that follow "Quick Tricks with a Loaf of Bread," page 18, and select something as easy as White Mountain Loaf. Just brush the loaf with lots of soft butter and roll it in flour. Place it on a cookie sheet and let it rise and spread. You'll be thrilled with the old-fashioned look. For a round shape try Pan Bread, or make the long French-like Bread. After a little practice with these simple shapes, you're going to want to try Mix and Match Bread, using two kinds of bread dough.

White and whole wheat frozen bread doughs are the kinds most commonly found in supermarkets. Other special flavors of frozen bread dough are French, Italian, rye, pumpernickel, raisin, cinnamon, and sweet. These special flavors are not always available and may not be sold in your stores. Most of the recipes for bread loaves in this section call for the white dough. In many of the recipes another flavor could be used. Choose a flavor that you like.

## Baking Helps for Dinner Loaves

The best pan for the basic loaf is the 8½ x 4½ x 2½-inch pan. However, the 9⅝ x 5½ x 2¾-inch pan makes a nice loaf, too. It is not as high, but it is good for sandwiches and toasting. (In the recipes in this book, these two pans will be referred to as 8x4- or 9x5-inch pans.) If smaller pans are used, the risen loaf may bulge over the sides and even collapse in the center.

Rising temperature and the age of the bread dough determine how long it is going to take to rise. The important point is to let it rise until it appears light in texture and more than doubled in size. In bread loaf pans it is easy to tell when it has risen enough. In the 8x4-inch pan, it will be a good inch above the sides of the pan. In the 9x5-inch pan, it will be about three-quarters to one inch above the sides.

* For a loaf that is well browned all the way around, use a dull-finished metal or glass baking pan.

* The bread pan should be well greased on the sides as well as the bottom. The loaf will brown better and will not stick. A butter wrapper will not grease the pan well enough. You should be able to see the streaks of shortening. Use a solid vegetable shortening.

* Brushing shaped loaves of bread dough before baking with melted butter flavored with garlic or seasoned salt adds a rich crust and a special flavor to the bread.

* For a shiny, crisp crust, brush the loaf with an Egg Wash before letting it rise or just before baking. An Egg Wash is a mixture of equal amounts of slightly beaten egg or egg white and water. If 1 teaspoon water to 1 tablespoon egg is used, the crust will be even shinier. (Make scrambled egg with the extra egg.)

* For sesame seed crunchiness, brush the loaf after shaping with an Egg Wash and then sprinkle with sesame seed. Sprinkle generously because as the bread rises, the surface area increases.
* The baked loaf should have a deep golden color all the way around. The loaf will sound hollow when thumped with the knuckles or fingers. If underbaked, the loaf may collapse. If overbaked, it may shrink before it is removed from the oven.

## Hints for the Baked Loaf

* Remove baked bread from the pan right away. This prevents a soggy crust.
* For a soft, shiny crust, brush the baked loaf with soft or melted butter.
* Cool bread on a wire rack. Many kinds of loaves keep their shape better if placed on their sides to cool.
* Use a serrated (rough-edged) knife for slicing bread. Put the loaf on its side and cut back and forth with a sawing motion. Do not bear down. Guide the knife back and forth and let it do the cutting.
* To store baked bread, first let it cool completely. Then place in a tight bread storage container or a plastic bag. Putting bread in the refrigerator makes it dry out more quickly. Refrigerate bread only if the weather is hot and humid or if the bread is to be kept several days.
* Home-baked bread makes great toast. Slice the bread after it has cooled, and then place it in a plastic bag and freeze. The frozen slices can be popped into the toaster.

## Quick Tricks with a Loaf of Bread Dough

The next five recipes require little or no skill. You do not need to wait for the dough to thaw to get it ready for baking. The results are beautiful. As the dough rises and bakes on the cookie sheet or in a large pan, it spreads out and takes on a neat look. It's crusty and crunchy all the way around. It's what we imagine the breads of long ago looked like—breads baked before there were bread pans, breads that were carefully and quickly slipped into the hearth on a long-handled wooden paddle.

Be sure you have read "Special Know-How for Baking with Frozen Dough," page 11, before you start to bake.

## Hearth Bread

*A special crusty bread—looks just like the loaf of bread baked in Grandmother's wood range, but so much easier.*

**Bake: 375° F. for 30 to 35 minutes    Makes: 1 loaf**

- 1 tablespoon egg
- 1 teaspoon water
- 1 loaf frozen white (honey wheat, French, or Italian) bread dough
  sesame seed
  cornmeal

Combine egg with water; brush top half of frozen loaf with mixture and sprinkle generously with sesame seed. Place on greased cookie sheet sprinkled with cornmeal. Cover; let rise in warm place until very light or doubled in size. (A frozen loaf will take from 4 to 6 hours to rise, depending on rising temperature. See bread dough label for more information.)

Bake at 375° F. for 30 to 35 minutes.

## White Mountain Loaf

*This billowy white cloud-like loaf is full of all kinds of old-fashioned goodness.*

**Bake: 375°F. for 30 to 35 minutes     Makes: 1 loaf**

- **1 loaf frozen white bread dough, partially thawed (French or Italian bread dough works well, too)**
- **soft or melted butter or margarine**
- **flour**

Brush top half of loaf generously with butter. Roll in flour to coat generously. Place on greased cookie sheet. Cover; let rise in warm place until very light or doubled in size. (A partially frozen loaf will take from 3 to 5 hours, depending on the rising temperature.)

Bake at 375° F. for 30 to 35 minutes.

## Butter Crust Vienna Bread

*Butter seeps into the crust to make bread extra light and give it a country fresh flavor.*

**Bake: 375° F. for 30 to 35 minutes     Makes: 1 loaf**

- **1 loaf frozen white (or French or Italian) bread dough, partially thawed**
- **2 tablespoons butter or margarine**

Place loaf on greased cookie sheet. Make a cut with sharp knife, ½-inch deep, lengthwise down center of loaf. Cut butter into thin slices and place in cut. Cover; let rise in warm place until very light and more than doubled in size, 2 to 3 hours.

Bake at 375° F. for 30 to 35 minutes. Brush with more butter, if desired.

## Oatmeal Wheat Bread

*A special wheat bread with a crunchy oatmeal crust. Great for grilled cheese sandwiches.*

**Bake: 375° F. for 30 to 35 minutes    Makes: 1 loaf**

  1 loaf frozen honey wheat dough
    milk
    rolled oats

Brush the loaf of frozen dough with milk (all the way around). Generously sprinkle with (or roll in) rolled oats. Place in well-greased bread loaf pan. Cover; let rise in warm place until doubled in size. (See bread dough label for time.)

Bake at 375° F. for 30 to 35 minutes.

*Grilled Cheese Sandwich:* (Day-old bread is easier to slice for sandwiches and toast.) Use 2 slices *bread* for each sandwich. Place a slice or two of *cheese* in between the bread slices. Lightly *butter* the outside of the sandwich on both sides. Heat a skillet or griddle over medium heat. Brown sandwich slowly on both sides until golden brown and the cheese melts. Serve immediately.


## Pan Bread

*It's easy to make and fun to serve. Take the loaf of bread to the table on a bread board and let each person slice off a chunk of warm bread. Great with steak or hamburger!*

**Bake: 375° F. for 30 to 35 minutes    Makes: 1 round loaf**

  1 loaf frozen bread dough (white, honey wheat, French, or other flavor), thawed

Shape thawed dough into a round loaf; place in greased 9-inch round pan. (Or divide in half; shape into balls and place in 2 greased 8-inch pans.) Cover; let rise in warm place until light or doubled in size, 1½ to 2 hours.

Bake at 375° F. for 30 to 35 minutes.

Quick Trick: Brush top with an equal amount of egg or egg white and water; sprinkle with sesame seed, if desired. Make several shallow cuts across the top to make an X or a checkerboard pattern. The cuts, in addition to making the loaf attractive, help to prevent cracking as the dough rises or expands.

## How to Shape Bread Dough

A good way to start shaping bread dough is to make An Old-Fashioned Loaf. It will give you the feel of the dough, a chance to watch the dough rise and see it bake, and a taste of how good home-baked bread really is. When you have mastered the technique of shaping and baking this loaf, you will be ready to try any of the recipes in this book. To help you further, the first recipe in each section has been described in detail in a step-by-step method. If you need answers to other bread-baking questions, look for them in the section, "Special Know-How for Baking with Frozen Dough," page 11, and "Baking Helps for Dinner Loaves," page 16 in this section.

## An Old-Fashioned Loaf

*(Step-by-Step Method)*

1. Remove frozen loaf of dough from the package. (Immediately reseal the package, pressing out as much air as possible. Return to freezer.)

2. Place dough in plastic bag to thaw and rise until it appears light and almost doubled in size. (The time needed will vary with the temperature. The warmer the place, the shorter the time. At room temperature, the total time will be 4 to 5 hours. If you plan ahead, place the dough in the refrigerator to thaw the night or morning before you bake it. See page 11 for more information on thawing and letting dough rise.)

3. Place the risen dough on a lightly floured board or rolling surface. Roll out to a 15x7-inch rectangle. Roll up tightly, starting with the 7-inch end. Seal dough with heels of hands after each roll. Seal bottom and ends.

4. When the loaf is all rolled up, pinch the overlap against the loaf to seal. This is the bottom, or seam side, of the loaf. Seal the ends by pressing down with side of hand and tuck ends under loaf.

5. Grease an 8x4-inch or a 9x5-inch bread pan on bottom and sides. (Streaks of grease should be visible.) Place shaped loaf, seam-side down, in pan.

6. Cover loosely with plastic wrap or by placing in large plastic bag. (Or use oven method described on page 11.) Set in warm place to rise until light and doubled in size. It will be 1 inch above the sides of the pan.

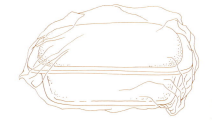

7. About 10 minutes before the bread is ready to bake, preheat the oven to 375° F. Bake at 375° F. until the bread is a rich golden brown, 30 to 35 minutes.

8. Immediately remove the bread from the pan and place on wire rack to cool. (It is important to remove the bread from the pan right away to prevent the crust from getting soggy.)

Now that you have seen what happens when you bake a loaf of bread dough as it comes from the package and have tried shaping An Old-Fashioned Loaf, you are ready to come up with a new shape of bread. The shape of the pan can shape the bread. Try baking a loaf in a special-shaped pan or casserole you find in your kitchen cabinets. The pan or dish you use should hold at least 6 cups, and 8 cups is better. To find out if a pan is the right size, see how many 1-cup measures of water it will hold. For a fancy touch, brush the loaf with seasoned butter or Egg Wash, page 103, and sprinkle it with sesame seed.

## Individual Loaves

*A loaf of bread for each person. If you don't have small loaf pans, make loaves round and bake in 5-inch foil pie pans.*

**Bake: 375° F. for 20 to 25 minutes     Makes: 6 small loaves**

   1 loaf frozen white (or honey wheat) bread dough, thawed

Divide dough into 6 parts. To shape into small loaves, flatten each piece of dough to a 6x3-inch rectangle. Roll up, starting with a 3-inch end. Pinch bottom and ends to seal. Place in well-greased 4½x2½-inch pans. (Or place 3 small loaves, crosswise, in regular bread loaf pan.) Cover; let rise in warm place until very light or doubled in size, 1 to 1½ hours.

Bake at 375° F. for 20 to 25 minutes.

## French-like Bread

*A long, skinny loaf of bread immediately says French bread. The French like lots of crust, and wheats grown in France make their tender yet crusty bread. To serve, cut diagonally (on a slant) into thick slices, brush with butter, wrap in foil, and heat in 350° F. oven 10 to 15 minutes.*

**Bake: 375° F. for 25 to 30 minutes    Makes: 1 loaf**

- 1 loaf frozen white (French or Italian) bread dough, thawed
- 2 tablespoons egg white
- 1 teaspoon water
  sesame seed or poppy seed, if desired

Let dough rise until almost doubled in size. Roll out on floured surface to a 15x7-inch rectangle. Roll up, starting with 15-inch side. Place diagonally on well-greased cookie sheet. Brush with egg white mixed with water; sprinkle with seed. With sharp knife, make 5 or 6 cuts across the top. Cover; let rise in warm place until very light or doubled in size, 1 to 1½ hours.

Bake at 375° F. for 25 to 30 minutes. For a crustier loaf, turn oven off and leave bread in oven 10 minutes.

Suggestion: To make a pizza with French-like Bread, follow the recipe on page 91.

## Raisin Bread

*Always a favorite—it makes great toast. Frozen white raisin bread dough is available. Make your own and add as many raisins as you like. It costs less, too.*

**Bake: 375° F. for 30 to 35 minutes    Makes: 1 loaf**

- 1 loaf frozen honey wheat (or white) bread dough, thawed
- ½ to 1 cup raisins

Let dough rise until light; then flatten to ½-inch. Sprinkle with raisins; fold in half. Roll out to a 15x7-inch rectangle. Roll up, starting with 7-inch side. Place in well-greased 8x4- or 9x5-inch pan. Cover; let rise in warm place until about 1 inch above sides of pan, 1 to 1½ hours.

Bake at 375° F. for 30 to 35 minutes.

Suggestion: After placing dough in pan, brush with melted butter and sprinkle with cinnamon sugar.

## Cheese Bubble Loaf

*A dinner loaf made up of tiny bubbles that are filled with cubes of cheese. Serve it warm, and each person can pull off a bubble. Or slice it when cold and each piece will have a patchwork of cheese. Toasted, it tastes like a grilled cheese sandwich.*

**Bake: 375° F. for 30 to 35 minutes    Makes: 1 loaf**

- 1 loaf frozen white (or honey wheat) bread dough, thawed
- 36 (½-inch) cubes Cheddar or Colby cheese

Divide dough into thirds; then divide each third into 12 pieces. Shape each piece around a cube of cheese, pinching to seal. Layer balls in a well-greased 9x5-inch pan. Cover; let rise in warm place until dough fills the pan, 1½ to 2 hours.

Bake at 375° F. for 30 to 35 minutes. Refrigerate leftover bread.

## Golden Crown

*This twisted crown is so pretty you will want to cut it at the dinner table.*

**Bake: 375° F. for 25 to 30 minutes    Makes: 1 large ring**

- 1 loaf frozen white (or honey wheat) bread dough, thawed
- 1 tablespoon egg or egg white
- 1 teaspoon water

Let dough rise until doubled in size. Divide in half. Shape each half into a 24-inch strip. Twist the two strips together loosely. Place on greased cookie sheet in a ring, sealing ends together. Combine egg and water; brush on bread. Cover; let rise in warm place until light or doubled in size, 30 to 60 minutes.

Bake at 375° F. for 25 to 30 minutes.

Tip: For an added touch, insert about 15 blanched whole almonds into twist before baking.

## Triple Treat Loaf

*Three small loaves, each with a different flavor, baked in the same pan. Nice for a small family, when you want one loaf for a meal. The others can be frozen for another time.*

**Bake: 375° F. for 30 to 35 minutes    Makes: 3 small loaves**

- 1 loaf frozen honey wheat bread dough, thawed
- ¼ cup raisins
- 1 teaspoon grated orange peel
- 1 teaspoon caraway seed
- 1 teaspoon anise seed

Divide dough into 3 parts. Flatten one part and sprinkle with raisins and peel; fold over and shape into small loaf, distributing fruit. Place crosswise in 8x4- or 9x5-inch well-greased pan. Work caraway into one remaining part and anise into the other. Shape into small loaves. Place crosswise in same pan. Cover; let rise in warm place until about 1 inch above sides of pan, 1 to 1½ hours.

Bake at 375° F. for 30 to 35 minutes. To serve, separate into small loaves.

## Honey Bee Twist

*Honey butter and a twist of nutmeg enhance this twisted loaf. Makes a good breakfast bread.*

**Bake: 350° F. for 30 to 35 minutes    Makes: 1 round loaf**

- 1 loaf frozen white (or honey wheat) bread dough, thawed
- 2 tablespoons soft butter or margarine
- 2 tablespoons honey
- ⅛ teaspoon nutmeg

Let dough rise until almost doubled in size. Shape into a 24-inch strip on floured surface. Starting in center and keeping dough flat, coil into a well-greased 9-inch round pan. Combine butter, honey, and nutmeg; brush over dough. Cover; let rise in warm place until light or doubled in size, 45 to 60 minutes.

Bake at 350° F. for 30 to 35 minutes. Remove from pan immediately.

## Bubble Dinner Bread

*Bubbles of bread are coated with cheese. Serve it warm, and each person can pull off a bubble. Slice loaf when served cold. Makes a good snack, too.*

**Bake: 375° F. for 30 to 35 minutes     Makes: 1 loaf**
- 1 **loaf frozen white bread dough, thawed**
- ¼ **cup butter or margarine, melted**
- ½ **cup grated Parmesan cheese**

Divide dough into 24 pieces. Using fork, coat each piece with butter, then cheese. Place bubbles in well-greased bundt pan, a 2-quart casserole, or a 9x5-inch pan. Cover; let rise in a warm place until very light or doubled in size, 1½ to 2 hours.

Bake at 375° F. for 30 to 35 minutes, or until deep golden brown. Remove from pan immediately.

## Mix and Match Bread

*(Two-Tone Swirl)*

*White and dark doughs are shaped together to give a variety of patterns in each slice of bread.*

**Bake: 375° F. for 30 to 35 minutes      Makes: 2 loaves**

- 1 loaf frozen white bread dough, thawed
- 1 loaf frozen honey wheat (or pumpernickel) bread dough, thawed

Let dough rise until almost doubled in size. Divide each loaf in half. Roll out part of each loaf to a 15x7-inch rectangle. Place white dough on top of honey wheat dough. Roll up tightly, sealing with heels of hands. Seal ends. Place seam-side down in well-greased 8x4- or 9x5-inch pan. Repeat with remaining dough. Cover; let rise in warm place until about 1 inch above sides of pans, 1 to 1½ hours.

Bake at 375° F. for 30 to 35 minutes.

### More Mix and Match Ideas:

*Half 'N Half Bread:* Divide each loaf in half. Shape into 8-inch strips. Place a white and honey wheat strip side by side in each pan.

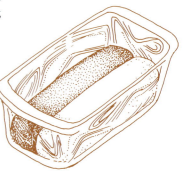

*Checkered Loaf:* Divide each loaf into fourths. Shape into 8-inch strips. Place a white and honey wheat strip side by side in each pan. Top each with a second strip, alternating flavors.

## Cinnamon Swirl Bread

*Always a favorite for toasting, or try one of the other suggested swirls for something different.*

**Bake: 375° F. for 30 to 35 minutes    Makes: 1 loaf**

- 1 loaf frozen white bread dough, thawed
- 2 tablespoons sugar
- 1½ teaspoons cinnamon
- ½ cup raisins

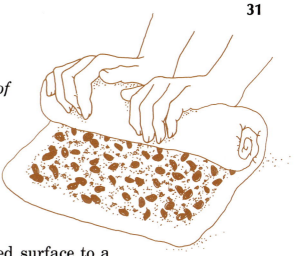

Let dough rise slightly. Roll out on floured surface to a 15x7-inch rectangle. Sprinkle with a mixture of the sugar, cinnamon, and raisins; press down firmly. Roll up tightly, starting with 7-inch side and sealing after each turn. Place in well-greased 8x4- or 9x5-inch pan. Cover; let rise in warm place until about 1 inch above the sides of pan, 1 to 1½ hours.

Bake at 375° F. for 30 to 35 minutes.

### Swirl Variations:

Leave out the cinnamon, sugar, and raisins, and try one of the swirl ideas listed below:

*Cheese Swirl:* 1 cup shredded *Cheddar cheese* and 1 teaspoon *poppy seed*.

*Peanut Butter Swirl:* ½ cup *peanut butter*.

Hint: When making pinwheel or swirl loaves, it is important to avoid air spaces while rolling up. Roll tightly and press out air bubbles that may form.

# Dinner Rolls

Slices or chunks of bread are great with any meal, but a warm dinner roll adds a special touch. A large, home-baked bun makes any sandwich special, too. The easy way to have homemade rolls is to start with a loaf of frozen bread dough (any flavor). One loaf of bread will make 12 large to 24 medium small rolls. For an extra touch, brush dinner rolls before baking with an Egg Wash, page 103, and sprinkle with sesame or poppy seed.

Several companies make a frozen dinner roll. Because they are small, frozen rolls thaw quickly, so if you're in a hurry, start with the frozen roll. The frozen dinner rolls cost more than a loaf of frozen white dough.

These rolls can be used to make Pan Rolls, Finger Rolls, Cloverleaf Rolls, and White Mountain Rolls. Other recipes that can start with frozen dinner rolls are Hamburger Hearth Buns, Butter Crumb Rolls, Peanut Butter Secrets, Hamburger Buns, Frankfurter Buns, and Hero Buns. You may want to try using them for some of the other shaping and flavor variations given in this section.

Be sure you have read "Special Know-How for Baking with Frozen Dough," page 11, before you start to bake.

## Thawing and Rising

If you wish, you can put the dough in the refrigerator the night or morning before and shape it about 1½ to 2 hours before it is time to bake. Or let it thaw at room temperature the day you make the rolls. For dinner rolls that can be shaped without rolling out the dough, you do not have to let the dough rise. Once the dough is thawed, it can be divided and shaped. The recipe will say if thawing only is enough or if the dough should rise. If the recipe says to let the dough rise slightly, let it rise just until it feels soft to the touch. Dough that has risen to double its size will rise much faster after shaping.

## Dividing Dough for Rolls

The easy way to divide dough into equal pieces is to cut the dough in half first and then cut the halves in half. Next cut each of these pieces into one-fourth of the number called for in the recipe. Or, if the number of pieces needed for the recipe is divisible by 3, start by dividing the whole piece into thirds.

## Reheating Baked Rolls

Warm rolls taste better. Make them early and reheat just before serving, using one of the methods listed below.

* If rolls are frozen, allow an extra 15 minutes for thawing.
* Wrap rolls in foil and heat in 350° F. oven 15 minutes.
* Place rolls in brown paper bag sprinkled with a few drops of water; heat 15 minutes at 350° F.
* Place rolls on a rack in skillet; put a few tablespoons water in skillet. Cover and steam about 10 minutes.
* Heat rolls in a bun warmer.

\* A microwave oven takes only seconds to reheat rolls. Place them on a paper plate to heat and cover with paper towel or waxed paper. Microwave 10 to 15 seconds per roll, and heat only as many as you need. Remember that overheating will cause rolls to dry out and become tough. After heating, let rolls stand for a few seconds so they will be evenly heated. The rolls are always hotter on the inside. Frozen rolls will take about twice as long to heat.

## Dinner Rolls

*(Step-by-Step Method)*

1. Place loaf of frozen dough in plastic bag to thaw.
2. Divide thawed dough into 12 to 24 pieces, depending on size of roll desired. (To divide, cut loaf in half; then cut each half in half. You now have 4 pieces. Cut each piece into one-fourth of the total number called for in the recipe.)

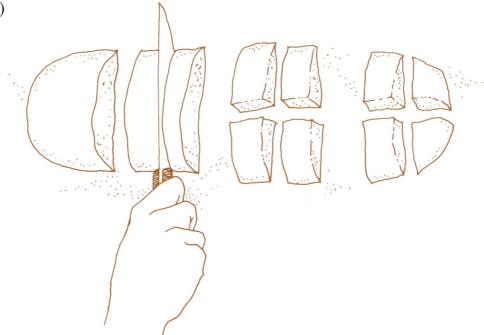

3. Shape each piece into ball by placing dough under palm of hand on a very lightly floured surface. (Breadboard works best. Do not use pastry cloth.) Cup your hand so your fingers and thumb just touch the dough. Using a circular motion and the fingers to help rotate the dough, move the dough until a smooth ball forms.

4. For a roll that is crusty all the way around, place shaped balls 2 inches or more apart on greased cookie sheet. For soft sides, place the rolls close together.

5. Cover loosely with plastic wrap or slip into a large plastic bag. Let rise in warm place until very light and more than doubled in size, 45 to 60 minutes.

6. Preheat oven to 400° F. about 10 minutes before rolls are ready for baking. Remove covering and bake rolls for 12 to 15 minutes, or until a rich golden brown. Cool on wire rack.

## Dinner Rolls

*Vary dinner rolls by varying the shape.*

**Bake: 400° F. for 12 to 15 minutes    Makes: 12 to 24 rolls**

  **1 loaf frozen bread dough (any flavor), thawed**

Shape dough as given below. Rising time will be longer if the dough is cold or has not risen before shaping. If shaping directions say to roll dough out, let it rise until it is double in size before shaping. Place shaped rolls on a greased cookie sheet or in a greased pan. Cover; let rise in warm place until light or doubled in size, 30 to 60 minutes.

Bake at 400° F. for 12 to 15 minutes, or as given below, until a rich golden brown. Brush warm rolls with butter.

### Shaping Directions:

*Dinner Buns:* Divide dough into 16 to 24 pieces. Shape into balls; flatten slightly. Place 2 inches apart on greased cookie sheet. (Rolls may also be baked in well-greased muffin cups.)

*Pan Rolls:* Divide dough into 16 to 24 pieces. Shape into balls. Place in rows in well-greased 9x9-, 10x8-, or 13x9-inch pan. Let rise and bake at 375° F. for 25 to 30 minutes. (Brush sides of balls of dough with *butter* for easy separation.)

*Finger Rolls:* Divide dough into 20 pieces. Shape each into 4-inch strips. *Butter* sides. Place in 2 rows in well-greased 10x8- or 9x9-inch pan. Let rise and bake at 375° F. for 25 to 30 minutes.

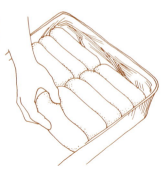

*Cloverleaf Rolls:* Divide dough into 12 pieces; and then divide each piece into thirds. Shape into balls; place 3 in each well-greased muffin cup.

*Crescents:* Divide dough in half. Roll out, half at a time, on floured surface to a 10-inch circle. Brush with melted *butter.* Cut into 8 or 9 wedges. Starting with wide end, roll each wedge to point. Place on greased cookie sheet, curving slightly, with point-side down.

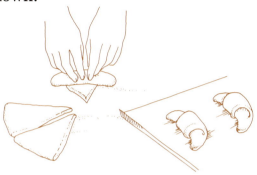

*White Mountain Rolls:* Divide dough into 16 pieces. Shape into balls; flatten slightly. Dip tops into melted *butter,* then *flour.* Place 2 inches apart on greased cookie sheet.

*Butter-Crust Rolls:* Divide dough into 12 to 16 pieces. Shape into round or oval balls. Place 2 inches apart on greased cookie sheet. With sharp knife, make a cut ¼-inch deep across tops. Place about ½ teaspoon *butter* in each cut.

## Double Quick Dinner Rolls

*If shaping rolls frightens you, then you're going to like these rolls; they need no shaping whatsoever.*

**Bake: 400° F. for 12 to 15 minutes     Makes: 12 to 18 rolls**

- 1 loaf frozen bread dough (any flavor), thawed
- 1 teaspoon egg
- 1 tablespoon water
- sesame seed or poppy seed

Divide dough into 12 to 18 pieces, depending on size and number of rolls desired. Place in well-greased muffin cups or about 2 inches apart on greased cookie sheet. Combine egg and water; brush tops of rolls. Sprinkle generously with sesame seed. Cover; let rise in warm place until light or doubled in size, 1½ to 2 hours.

Bake at 400° F. for 12 to 15 minutes.

## Hamburger Buns

*Freshly baked buns for hamburgers or frankfurters make an easy supper good enough for a company meal.*

**Bake: 400° F. for 12 to 15 minutes    Makes: 12 buns**

- **1 loaf frozen white bread dough, thawed (honey wheat, pumpernickel, Italian, and French frozen doughs make deluxe buns)**

Divide dough into 12 pieces. Shape into balls and flatten. Place 3 inches apart on greased cookie sheet. Cover; let rise in warm place until very light or doubled in size, 1 to 1½ hours.

Bake at 400° F. for 12 to 15 minutes.

*Super-Hamburger Buns:* Make 8 to 10 buns from a loaf. Flatten. Brush with a mixture of *egg* and a small amount of *water;* then sprinkle with *sesame seed.* Cut an X on the top.

*Frankfurter Buns:* Shape pieces of dough into buns about 4 inches long and 1 inch wide; flatten. Let rise and bake.

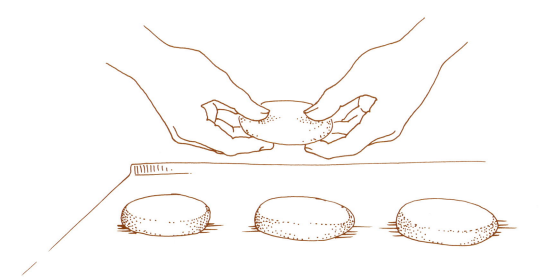

## Hamburger Hearth Buns

*A touch of the Old World makes fancy buns for hamburgers.*

**Bake: 400° F. for 12 to 15 minutes     Makes: 10 large buns**

   1 **loaf frozen white (French or Italian) bread dough, thawed**
     **melted butter or margarine**
     **flour**
     **seasoned salt**

Divide dough into 10 pieces. Shape into balls and flatten. Dip tops into butter and then into flour to coat generously. Place 3 inches apart on greased cookie sheet. Sprinkle with salt. Cover; let rise in warm place until light or doubled in size, 1 to 1½ hours.

Bake at 400° F. for 12 to 15 minutes. Use as hamburger buns or as buns for sandwich meats and cheeses.

## Oatmeal Wheat Rolls

*Wheat rolls coated all the way around with oatmeal.*

**Bake: 375° F. for 12 to 15 minutes     Makes: 12 large buns**

   1 **loaf frozen honey wheat (or white) bread dough, thawed**
     **milk**
     **rolled oats**

Divide dough into 12 pieces. Shape each into ball. Brush lightly all the way around with milk. Roll in oats; place in well-greased muffin cups. Cover; let rise in warm place until light or doubled in size, 1½ to 2 hours.

Bake at 375° F. for 12 to 15 minutes.

*Oatmeal Hamburger Wheat Buns:* Place shaped rolls 3 inches apart on greased cookie sheet and flatten. Let rise and bake.


## Hero Buns

*Large buns that make good submarine, torpedo, or poor boy sandwiches. A good summer supper after the baseball game. Fill rolls early and refrigerate.*

**Bake: 375° F. for 20 to 25 minutes     Makes: 6 or 8 rolls**

- 1 loaf frozen white (French or Italian) bread dough, thawed
- 1 tablespoon egg
- 1 tablespoon water
-   sesame or poppy seed

Divide dough into 6 or 8 pieces. Shape into oblong or round buns. Place 3 inches apart on greased cookie sheet. Make a cut or two across the top of each. Combine egg and water; brush on rolls. Sprinkle with seeds. Cover; let rise in warm place until light or doubled in size, 1 to 2 hours.

Bake at 375° F. for 20 to 25 minutes.

*To Serve:* Split, butter, and fill with lettuce, cold cuts of meat, cheese, pickles, and tomatoes. If you want to serve warm, leave out lettuce; wrap in foil and heat in 350° F. oven about 15 minutes.

*Other Good Fillings:* Egg or tuna salad; tuna and cheese, heated or broiled; beans and wieners; barbecued beef; sloppy Joe filling.

## Butter Crumb Rolls

*Crunchy coated buns that are great for sandwiches. Or make them bigger for hamburger buns.*

**Bake: 375° F. for 15 to 20 minutes     Makes: 12 rolls**

- 1 loaf frozen (any flavor) bread dough, thawed
- 1/3 cup bread crumbs (or ready-to-eat cereal, crushed)
- 1 teaspoon poppy seed, caraway, or mixed herbs
- 2 tablespoons butter or margarine, melted

Divide dough into 12 pieces. Shape into balls. Combine crumbs and seeds. Coat balls with butter, then crumbs. Place 3 inches apart on greased cookie sheet. Flatten slightly. Cover; let rise in warm place until light or doubled in size, 1 to 1½ hours.

Bake at 375° F. for 15 to 20 minutes.

**Short Cut Idea:** If you do not want to shape rolls, just dip pieces of dough into butter; then coat with crumbs.


## Honey Rolls

*Honey butter adds the final touch to these rolls.*

**Bake: 375° F. for 15 to 20 minutes     Makes: 18 rolls**

- 1 loaf frozen white (or honey wheat) bread dough, thawed
- 3 tablespoons butter or margarine, soft or melted nutmeg
- ¼ cup honey

Let dough rise until doubled in size. Roll out on floured surface to an 18x10-inch rectangle. Brush with half the butter; sprinkle lightly with nutmeg. Roll up, starting with 18-inch side. Cut into 18 pieces. Place, cut-side down, in well-greased muffin cups or 13x9-inch pan. Cover; let rise in warm place until very light or doubled in size, 30 to 45 minutes. Combine remaining butter and honey. Brush carefully over risen rolls.

Bake at 375° F. for 15 to 20 minutes. Remove from pan immediately.

## Peanut Butter Secrets

*Rolls stuffed with peanut butter make a great after-school treat.*

**Bake: 400° F. for 12 to 15 minutes    Makes: 20 rolls**

- 1 **loaf frozen white (or honey wheat) bread dough, thawed**
- **peanut butter**

Let dough rise slightly. Divide into 20 pieces. Flatten each piece and top with a teaspoonful peanut butter. Bring dough around filling. Seal and shape into ball. Place 2 inches apart on greased cookie sheet. Cover; let rise in warm place until light or doubled in size, 1 to 1½ hours.

Bake at 400° F. for 12 to 15 minutes.

*Peanut Au Chocolat Secrets* Pieces of chocolate candy inside rolls used to be a favorite treat for French children when they came home from school. Peanut butter and chocolate inside these secret rolls will become a special treat for you too. Seal 3 or 4 *semi-sweet chocolate pieces* inside rolls with the peanut butter

# Sweet Rolls

Another favorite bread is the sweet roll. Sweet rolls are popular for breakfast, with milk at midmorning, or as an afterschool snack. Danish bakers are famous for their tender, light, and flaky rich sweet rolls, often referred to as Danish pastry. The cinnamon roll, our most popular roll, comes to us from Sweden. In American bakeries and homes we have adapted these famous Old World rolls to our taste and have invented different combinations and shapes.

A frozen sweet dough is sold in some supermarkets. If you can't find it, ask your grocer if it is available. Frozen raisin dough can also be used to make sweet rolls. The basic white dough costs less than these special doughs, and it can be used for any of the recipes in this section.

Many different kinds of sweet rolls can be made from a loaf of basic white dough. The all-time favorite cinnamon roll, for instance, comes in several types and shapes. It can be flat and crispy, high and light with soft sides, crunchy with cinnamon sugar, or gooey like a caramel roll.

If you're looking for something to start with, try Cinnamon Buns, page 52. There's no shaping. All you do is cut off a piece of dough, coat it with butter and cinnamon sugar, and place it in a muffin cup to rise. The step-by-step method for making Mom's Cinnamon Rolls, page 49, will show you how to shape sweet rolls. They're delicious, but don't stop there. In this section there are lots of recipes for sweet rolls that look fancy but are easy to make. Surprise your family with something brand-new.

## Hints for Making Sweet Rolls

If you're making sweet rolls after school, take the dough out of the freezer the night or morning before and let it thaw in the refrigerator. If you're going to roll it out, let it stand at room temperature at least one hour to warm and rise to about double in size. Any dough that is to be rolled out is easier to handle if it has doubled in size.

Be sure you have read "Special Know-How for Baking with Frozen Dough," page 11, before you start to bake.

* To bake sweet rolls on cookie sheets, line them with foil and then grease. This makes clean-up easier.

* The easy way to divide dough into equal pieces is to cut the dough in half first and then cut the halves in half. Next cut each of these pieces into one-fourth of the number called for in the recipe. Or, if the number of pieces needed for the recipe is divisible by 3, start by dividing the whole piece into thirds.

* When there are scraps of dough to reroll, stack them and then roll them out to the needed thickness. Or you may want to shape these small pieces of dough into a dinner roll or two.

* To dust rolls or coffee cake with powdered sugar, place sugar in small strainer and press through with finger or spoon. This prevents lumps and lets you dust evenly.

## Mom's Cinnamon Rolls

*(Step-by-Step Method)*

1. Let dough rise in a plastic bag until doubled in size.

2. Meanwhile, butter a 9x9- or 10x8-inch pan well on the bottom and sides. Sprinkle with ½ cup chopped nuts, if desired.

3. Place risen dough on a lightly floured surface. *Do not rework the dough into a ball.* (Preferably use a wooden board or a formica surface. Do not use a pastry cloth for rolling bread dough.)

4. Roll and stretch the dough into a 15x10-inch rectangle, turning the dough over if necessary.

5. Brush dough with 3 tablespoons soft butter or margarine. Sprinkle with 3 tablespoons each granulated and brown sugar; then sprinkle with 1 teaspoon cinnamon.

6. Roll up, starting with 15-inch side.

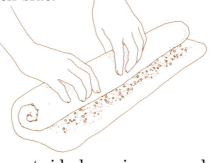

7. Cut into 12 to 16 pieces. Place, cut-side down, in prepared pan.

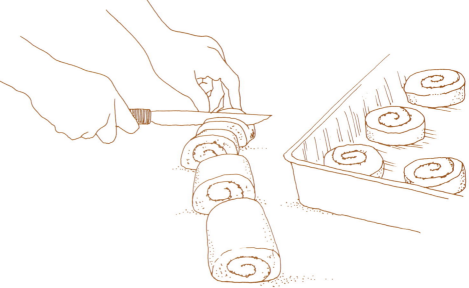

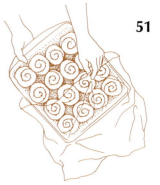

8. Cover loosely with plastic wrap, waxed paper, or large plastic bag. Let rise in warm place until light or doubled in size, 30 to 60 minutes.

9. Bake at 375° F. for 20 to 25 minutes, or until light golden brown. Immediately turn out on wire rack.

## Mom's Cinnamon Rolls

*These lightly carameled cinnamon rolls were developed from the rolls my mother used to make for a special Sunday treat.*

Bake: 375° F. for 20 to 25 minutes    Makes: 12 to 16 rolls

- 1 loaf frozen white (or sweet) bread dough, thawed
- ½ cup chopped nuts, if desired
- 3 tablespoons butter or margarine, melted
- 3 tablespoons granulated sugar
- 3 tablespoons brown sugar
- 1 teaspoon cinnamon

Let dough rise until doubled in size. Sprinkle nuts into buttered 9x9- or 10x8-inch pan. Roll out dough on floured surface to a 15x10-inch rectangle. Brush with butter; sprinkle with remaining ingredients. Roll up, starting with 15-inch side. Cut into 12 to 16 pieces. Place, cut-side down, in pan. Cover; let rise in warm place until light or doubled in size, 30 to 60 minutes.

Bake at 375° F. for 20 to 25 minutes, or until light golden brown. Immediately turn out onto rack.

## Cinnamon Buns

*You'll like to make these easy cinnamon rolls—no rolling.*

**Bake: 375° F. for 15 to 20 minutes       Makes: 18 rolls**

- 1 loaf frozen white (or sweet) bread dough, thawed
- ½ cup sugar
- ¼ cup finely chopped nuts
- 1 teaspoon cinnamon
- ¼ cup butter or margarine, melted

Divide dough into 18 pieces. Combine sugar, nuts, and cinnamon. Roll in butter and then in sugar mixture. Place in well-greased muffin cups. Cover; let rise in warm place until light or doubled in size, about 1½ hours.

Bake at 375° F. for 15 to 20 minutes. Remove from pans immediately. If desired, frost with Vanilla Icing, page 102.

*Butterscotch Nut Buns:* Place ¼ teaspoon *water* in each well-greased muffin cup, then 1 teaspoon chopped *nuts*. Melt ¼ cup *butter*. Combine ¼ cup *granulated sugar,* ¼ cup *brown sugar,* and ½ teaspoon *cinnamon*. Coat pieces of dough first with butter and then sugar mixture. Place on top of the nuts. Let rise and bake.

*Orange Buns:* Place 1 teaspoon *orange juice* in each well-greased muffin cup. Melt ¼ cup *butter*. Combine ½ cup *sugar,* 1 tablespoon grated *orange peel,* and ¼ cup *coconut,* if desired. Coat pieces of dough first with butter and then with orange-sugar mixture. Let rise and bake.

Suggestion: If desired, any of the above rolls may be baked in a well-greased 9x9-, 10x8-, or 13x9-inch pan. For the Butterscotch Buns, sprinkle 1 tablespoon water in pan; for the Orange Buns, ¼ cup orange juice.

## Caramel Nut Rolls

*The old-fashioned gooey pecan roll is always a favorite. Please the family by making these tasty rolls.*

**Bake: 375° F. for 25 to 30 minutes      Makes: 15 or 16 rolls**

- 1 loaf frozen white (or sweet) bread dough, thawed
- 4 tablespoons butter or margarine, melted
- ½ cup brown sugar
- 2 teaspoons water
- 2 tablespoons light corn syrup
- ½ cup broken pecans or walnuts
- ½ teaspoon cinnamon

Let dough rise until doubled in size. Brush a 10x8- or 9x9-inch pan with 1 tablespoon butter. Combine 2 tablespoons butter, ¼ cup brown sugar, water, and corn syrup. Spread in pan. Sprinkle with pecans. Roll out dough on floured surface to a 16x12-inch rectangle. Brush with remaining butter and sprinkle with ¼ cup brown sugar and cinnamon. Roll up, starting with 16-inch side. Cut into 15 or 16 pieces. Place, cut-side down, in pan. Cover; let rise in warm place until light, 30 to 60 minutes.

Bake at 375° F. for 25 to 30 minutes. Cool 1 minute. Loosen edges and turn out onto wire rack lined with waxed paper.

## Elephant Ears

*Now you can make this favorite thin, sugary-crisp bakery roll.*

**Bake: 375° F. for 15 to 18 minutes     Makes: 16 rolls**

- 1 loaf frozen white (or sweet) bread dough, thawed
- 3 tablespoons butter or margarine, melted
- ¾ cup sugar
- 2 tablespoons brown sugar
- 2 teaspoons cinnamon

Let dough rise until doubled in size. Combine sugars and cinnamon. Roll out dough on floured surface to a 16x12-inch rectangle. Brush with half the butter and sprinkle with 2 tablespoons of the sugar mixture. Fold in half; roll out again to 16x12-inch rectangle. Brush with remaining butter and sprinkle with 2 tablespoons of the sugar mixture. Roll up, starting with 16-inch side. Cut into 16 pieces. Sprinkle rolling surface with sugar mixture. Roll out each piece to ⅛ to ¼ inch thick, turning to coat both sides with sugar. Place on well-greased cookie sheets. Let rise 15 minutes.

Bake at 375° F. for 15 to 18 minutes.

*Danish Butter Crispies:* Omit brown sugar and decrease cinnamon to ½ teaspoon. Add ½ cup *almond slices* to the sugar mixture.

## Danish Rolls

*You'll like these rolls—they look just like the jelly-topped rolls you buy in a bake shop.*

**Bake: 375° F. for 15 to 20 minutes       Makes: 12 rolls**

- 1 loaf frozen white (or sweet) bread dough, thawed
- 1 tablespoon butter or margarine, melted
- ½ Sugar Streusel recipe, page 103
- 1 tablespoon beaten egg
- 2 teaspoons milk
- jam, jelly, or fruit pie filling

Let dough rise until almost doubled in size. Roll out on floured surface to a 12-inch square. Brush with butter; then cut into 1-inch strips. Twist each strip many times and coil onto greased cookie sheet, keeping flat. Cover; let rise in warm place until light or doubled in size, 30 to 60 minutes.

Combine egg and milk. Brush carefully over rolls. Sprinkle each with a teaspoonful of Streusel.

Bake at 375° F. for 15 minutes. Place a spoonful of jam in center of each. Bake 3 to 5 minutes. Frost with an icing, page 102, if desired.

*Danish "S" Rolls:* Twist strips from above recipe; place in "s" shape, with sides touching, on greased cookie sheet. Let rise, brush with *egg mixture,* sprinkle with *Streusel,* and place *lemon pie filling* or *jelly* along center strip. Bake and frost.

## Grandma's Raisin Sugar Rolls

*A touch of sweetness and lots of raisins will make this old-fashioned roll one of your favorites.*

**Bake: 375° F. for 20 to 25 minutes     Makes: 15 or 16 rolls**

- 1 loaf frozen white (or sweet) bread dough, thawed
- 2 tablespoons butter or margarine, melted
- ¼ cup sugar
- ¼ teaspoon cinnamon or nutmeg
- ½ cup raisins

Let dough rise until doubled in size. Roll out on floured surface to a 15x10-inch rectangle. Brush with butter; sprinkle with remaining ingredients. Roll up, starting with 15-inch side. Cut into 15 or 16 rolls. Place, cut-side down, in well-buttered 9x9- or 10x8-inch pan. Cover; let rise in warm place until light or doubled in size, 30 to 60 minutes.

Bake at 375° F. for 20 to 25 minutes, or until light golden brown. Remove from pan immediately. Frost rolls with one of the icings on page 102.

## Jelly Rolls

*Swirls of jelly make these good lunch or breakfast rolls. For a peanut butter and jelly sandwich, try the variation.*

**Bake: 375° F. for 15 to 18 minutes     Makes: 18 rolls**

- 1 loaf frozen white (sweet or honey wheat) bread dough, thawed
- 1 tablespoon soft or melted butter
- ½ cup preserves, jelly, or marmalade
- 2 tablespoons bread or graham cracker crumbs

Let dough rise until doubled in size. Roll out on floured surface to an 18x10-inch rectangle. Brush with butter, then preserves. Sprinkle with crumbs. Roll up, starting with 18-inch side. Cut into 18 pieces. Place, cut-side down, in well-greased muffin cups. Cover; let rise in warm place until light or doubled in size, 30 to 60 minutes.

Bake at 375° F. for 15 to 18 minutes. Loosen and turn out immediately.

Note: Rolls may be baked in greased 13x9-inch pan. Bake 20 to 25 minutes.

*Peanut Butter Jelly Rolls:* Combine ¼ cup *peanut butter* and ¼ cup *jelly;* substitute for preserves in above recipe.

## Orange Sticky Rolls

*A good roll to serve for a Sunday brunch.*

**Bake: 375° F. for 20 to 25 minutes     Makes: 15 or 16 rolls**

- 1 loaf frozen white (sweet or honey wheat) bread dough, thawed
- 2 tablespoons butter or margarine, melted
- ¼ cup sugar
- ¼ cup light corn syrup
- ¼ cup orange juice
- 1 tablespoon soft butter or margarine
- 1 tablespoon grated orange peel
- ⅛ teaspoon nutmeg or mace

Let dough rise until doubled in size. Combine melted butter, sugar, syrup, and juice. Spread in well-buttered 10x8- or 9x9-inch pan. Roll out dough on floured surface to a 15x12-inch rectangle. Brush with soft butter; sprinkle with peel and nutmeg. Roll up, starting with 15-inch side. Cut into 15 or 16 pieces. Place, cut-side down, in prepared pan. Cover; let rise in warm place until light or doubled in size, 30 to 60 minutes.

Bake at 375° F. for 20 to 25 minutes. Loosen edges immediately and turn onto wire rack over waxed paper.

**Suggestion:** For flatter and more crusty rolls, use a 13x9-inch pan. Cut the 15-inch roll into 18 or 20 pieces and place in the prepared pan.

## Marshmallow Nuggets

*A sweet touch hides inside each of these rolls—fun party rolls.*

**Bake: 375° F. for 15 to 18 minutes      Makes: 18 rolls**

- 1 loaf frozen white dough, thawed
- 18 regular marshmallows
- 1 tablespoon sugar
- ¼ teaspoon cinnamon
- 2 tablespoons butter or margarine, melted

Let dough rise until almost doubled in size. Divide into 18 pieces. Flatten each piece and shape around a marshmallow. Pinch together well on the bottom to seal. Place seam-side down in greased muffin cups or a greased 13x9-inch pan. Combine sugar and cinnamon. Brush tops of rolls with butter; sprinkle with cinnamon sugar. Cover; let rise in warm place until light and doubled in size, 30 to 60 minutes.

Bake at 375° F. for 15 to 18 minutes in muffin cups; 20 to 25 minutes in the pan. Remove from pan immediately.

## Ranch-Style Cinnamon Rolls

*Giant-sized cinnamon rolls that will satisfy a hungry appetite.*

Bake: 375° F. for 15 to 20 minutes      Makes: 6 large rolls

- 1 loaf frozen white (or sweet) bread dough, thawed
- 3 tablespoons butter or margarine, melted
- 1/3 cup sugar
- 1 teaspoon cinnamon
- ¼ cup finely chopped nuts

Let dough rise until doubled in size. Roll out on floured surface to a 15x10-inch rectangle. Brush with most of the butter. Combine sugar, cinnamon, and nuts; sprinkle most over dough. Roll up, starting with 10-inch side. Cut into 6 pieces. Place 2 inches apart, on greased cookie sheet. Flatten to about ½ inch; brush with remaining butter and sprinkle with sugar mixture. Cover; let rise in warm place until light, 30 to 45 minutes.

Bake at 375° F. for 15 to 20 minutes. Frost warm rolls with a half-recipe of one of the icings on page 102.

# Coffee Cakes

Fancy, rich breads date back thousands of years. Animal-shaped breads were baked as sacrifices to offer to the gods of long ago. The eating of other special breads at holiday time also had religious meaning. People ate breads that we might call "coffee cakes" today long before they drank coffee, which first became a popular drink in Arabia in the 1200s.

Coffee cakes and breads laden with fruits most probably had their beginnings after the rise of bakeries throughout Europe. When baking became a business, shop owners tried to increase sales by trying new and fancier cakes and breads. During the Renaissance, a great flowering of the arts began in Italy and spread through Europe. Some bakers followed the times and became artists in their work. They competed to see who could make the most beautiful decorated bread. Today, chefs and bakers still compete in food shows, displaying their artistic skills.

Special breads baked in the home and in bakeries are not as beautiful as those made to show off an artist's skill, but they are just as good, and sometimes better, to eat. Coffee cakes and rich breads, even those carrying the old, old names, have greatly improved in quality. They can be simple to make and delicious, too.

Coffee cakes are as varied as any other type of bread. They may be coated with cinnamon or other flavored sugar, pressed into a pan, shaped into a loaf, rolled out and shaped, filled, or topped with a fruit filling. Coffee cake for breakfast, coffee cake for brunch, coffee cake for dessert, coffee cake for snacking—there's one for every occasion.

Making a coffee cake is foolproof when the dough is already made for you. Included in this section are old favorites adapted to frozen dough, as well as brand-new ideas. For a coffee cake that requires no shaping, follow the step-by-step directions for Streusel Coffee Cake, page 63. Press the dough in the pan, sprinkle with a butter crumb topping, and add icing while it's still warm from the oven.

Be sure you have read "Special Know-How for Baking with Frozen Dough," page 11, before you start to bake.

## Hints for Making Coffee Cakes

* Frozen sweet dough is very good for kuchens and streusel coffee cakes. If it is sold in supermarkets near you, try it.

* Be sure to let the loaf of dough rise until it is very light and is more than doubled in size. It is much easier to roll out. Do not knead the dough or handle it too much once it has risen because it will be hard to roll out. Just lay it on a floured surface and start rolling and stretching the dough to the size you need. Do not over-flour the surface. Some brands of frozen dough roll out more easily than others, thus making shaping easier.

* Some of the recipes require very little shaping, and the coffee cake can be made as soon as the dough is thawed. Follow recipe directions. Dough that does not rise before shaping needs a longer rising time after the coffee cake is made.

* To dust coffee cakes with powdered sugar, place sugar in a small strainer and press through with finger or spoon. This prevents lumps and lets you dust evenly.
* When coffee cakes are baked on cookie sheets, line sheets with foil and then grease. This will make cleanup easier.

## Streusel Coffee Cake

*(Step-by-Step Method)*

1. Place dough in plastic bag to thaw and rise until almost doubled in size.

2. Meanwhile, grease bottom and sides of 13x9-inch pan well. You should be able to see streaks of grease. Press dough into bottom of pan.

3. Mix ¾ cup flour with ½ cup sugar and ½ teaspoon cinnamon. Add ¼ cup soft butter or margarine. Cut the butter into the mixture with a fork until it makes fine crumbs. Sprinkle evenly over dough.

4. Cover with plastic wrap or waxed paper. Let rise in warm place until doubled in size, 45 to 60 minutes. The time needed for rising will depend on how much the dough had risen before it was pressed into the pan.

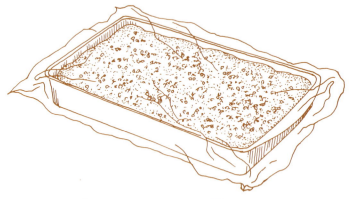

5. About 10 minutes before baking, preheat oven to 375° F. Bake 20 to 25 minutes, or until edges are golden brown. Do not remove from pan.

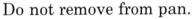

6. Cool in pan a few minutes and drizzle Vanilla Icing, page 102, back and forth over the top. Good served warm.

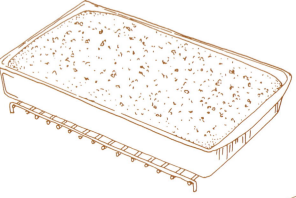

## Streusel Coffee Cake

*Your choice of some Old World coffee cakes.*
*A good substitute for cake.*

**Bake: 375° F. for 20 to 25 minutes    Makes 13x9-inch coffee cake**

- 1 loaf frozen white (or sweet) bread dough, thawed
- ½ cup sugar
- ¾ cup flour
- ¼ cup butter or margarine
- ½ teaspoon cinnamon

When dough is partially risen, press into well-greased 13x9-inch pan. Cut butter into remaining ingredients; sprinkle over dough. Cover; let rise in warm place until doubled in size, 45 to 60 minutes.

Bake at 375° F. for 20 to 25 minutes. Frost with Vanilla Icing, page 102.

Instead of topping in recipe, try one of the suggestions below.

*Dutch Sugar Cake:* Press dough into pan as directed. Let rise. Cut 2 tablespoons *butter* or *margarine* into ¼ cup *brown sugar;* ¼ cup *sugar,* ¼ cup *flour,* and 1 teaspoon *cinnamon*. Sprinkle dough with this mixture just before baking.

*Swedish Cinnamon Coffee Cake:* Combine ½ cup *sugar,* 2 tablespoons *butter* or *margarine,* and 2 teaspoons *cinnamon*. Sprinkle over dough. Let rise and bake.

## Apple Kuchen

*A coffee cake that comes to us from Germany.*

**Bake: 350° F. for 35 to 40 minutes    Makes: 13x9-inch coffee cake**

- 1 loaf frozen white (or sweet) bread dough, thawed
- 2 cups thinly sliced, pared apples
- 2 tablespons butter or margarine
- ½ cup sugar
- 1 teaspoon cinnamon
- 1 egg
- ¼ cup cream

Let dough rise slightly. Press into well-greased 13x9-inch pan. Arrange apples on top. Cut butter into sugar and cinnamon. Sprinkle over apples. Cover; let rise in warm place until doubled in size, 1 to 1½ hours.

Bake at 350° F. for 20 to 25 minutes, or until light golden brown. Beat egg and cream together until blended. Spoon over apples. Bake 10 to 15 minutes or until custard is set and apples are tender. Best the day baked.

Refrigerate leftover coffee cake. Reheat to serve.

## Monkey Bread

*One of the old, old favorite coffee cakes— bubbles of bread are coated with sugar- cinnamon mixture.*

**Bake: 350° F. for 35 to 40 minutes    Makes: 1 coffee cake**

- 1 loaf frozen white (or sweet) bread dough, thawed
- ½ cup sugar (half brown)
- 1 teaspoon cinnamon
- ½ cup coconut or chopped nuts, if desired
- ¼ cup butter or margarine, melted

Cut dough into 24 small pieces. Combine sugar, cinnamon,

and coconut. Coat dough pieces with butter; then roll in sugar mixture. Place in well-greased 9- or 12-cup bundt pan. Cover; let rise in warm place until light or doubled in size. 1½ to 2 hours.

Bake at 350° F. for 35 to 40 minutes. Cool 1 or 2 minutes. Then loosen edges and carefully turn out onto serving plate.

Note: Bread may be baked in 2 bread loaf pans or a tube pan with a solid bottom.

## Butterscotch Bubble Loaf

*A favorite coffee cake—butterscotch pudding mix coats bubbles of bread and makes a gooey, caramel-like mixture on the bottom.*

**Bake: 375° F. for 25 to 30 minutes     Makes: 1 coffee cake**

- 6 **tablespoons butter or margarine, melted**
- 10 **to 12 maraschino cherries, if desired**
- ½ **cup coconut or chopped nuts**
- 1 **loaf frozen white bread dough, partially thawed**
- 1 **package butterscotch pudding and pie filling mix (not instant)**
- ¼ **cup brown sugar**
- ½ **teaspoon cinnamon**

Generously butter 9- or 12-cup bundt pan or 9x9-inch pan. Arrange cherries on bottom. Sprinkle with coconut. Cut partially thawed dough into 24 pieces. Place pieces in pan. Sprinkle with pudding mix, brown sugar, and cinnamon. Drizzle with remaining butter. Cover; let rise in warm place until light or doubled in size, 3 to 4 hours.

Bake at 375° F. for 25 to 30 minutes. Let stand 30 to 60 seconds. Turn out onto plate or wire rack which has been lined with waxed paper.

## Frosty Snowball Cakes

*So simple! Tiny balls frosted while warm and sprinkled with nuts add a sweet touch.*

**Bake: 350° F. for 25 to 30 minutes    Makes: 2 (8 inch) coffee cakes**

    1 loaf frozen white (or sweet) bread dough, thawed
       Orange or Lemon Icing, page 102
       chopped nuts or coconut

Divide dough into 30 pieces. Place in 2 greased 9-inch pie pans or 8-inch round cake pans (15 pieces per pan). Cover; let rise in warm place until light or doubled in size, 1½ to 2 hours.

Bake at 350° F. for 25 to 30 minutes. Remove from pans. Frost warm cakes with half the icing. Cool; frost with remaining icing. Sprinkle with nuts.


## Swedish Tea Ring

*This festive coffee cake from Sweden is popular any time of the year. In Sweden it is called a Klippta Kransor, meaning "a cut dough." To us the most common filling is cinnamon and sugar, but any of the fillings below can be used.*

**Bake: 375° F. for 20 to 25 minutes    Makes: 1 round coffee cake**

    1 loaf frozen white (or sweet) bread dough, thawed
    1 tablespoon butter or margarine, soft or melted

Let dough rise until doubled in size. Prepare one of the fillings below. Roll out dough on floured surface to a 15x12-inch rectangle. Brush with butter; sprinkle or spread with filling. Roll up, starting with the 15-inch side. Form into a ring on well-greased cookie sheet; seal ends together. Make cuts ¾ inch apart, almost to center of ring. Turn cuts on sides. Cover; let rise in warm place until light or doubled in size, 30 to 60 minutes.

Bake at 375° F. for 20 to 25 minutes. Frost warm ring with Vanilla Icing, page 102.

Note: For easier pan washing, line cookie sheet with foil; then grease.

### Tea Ring Fillings:

*Cinnamon-Sugar Filling:* Combine 1/3 cup *sugar*, ¼ cup chopped *nuts, raisins*, or *coconut*, and 1 teaspoon *cinnamon*.

*Apple Filling:* Shred 2 pared *apples*. Combine with ¼ cup *sugar*, ¼ cup *raisins*, and ½ teaspoon *cinnamon*.

*Mincemeat Filling:* Use 1 cup prepared *mincemeat*.

*Christmas Filling:* Combine ¼ cup *sugar*, ½ teaspoon *cardamom*, ¼ cup *almond slices,* and ½ cup mixed *candied fruit*.

*Orange-Coconut Filling:* Combine ¼ cup *sugar*, ½ cup *coconut*, and 2 tablespoons grated *orange peel*.

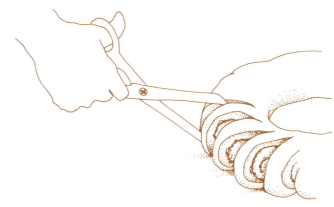

## Cinnamon Roll Coffee Cake

*Cinnamon rolls can be arranged in many ways to take on a special shape for a special day. A nice addition to the Christmas dinner.*

**Bake: 375° F. for 20 to 30 minutes    Makes: 1 or 2 coffee cakes**

- 1 loaf frozen white (or sweet) bread dough, thawed
- 2 tablespoons butter or margarine, melted
- 1/3 cup sugar
- 2 tablespoons graham cracker or bread crumbs
- 1 tablespoon brown sugar
- 1 teaspoon cinnamon

Let dough rise until doubled in size. Roll out on floured surface to a 16x12-inch rectangle. Brush with butter. Combine remaining ingredients; sprinkle all but about 1 tablespoon over dough. Roll up, starting with 16-inch side. Cut into 16 rolls and arrange as directed below. (Flatten rolls slightly before shaping into coffee cake.) Cover; let rise in warm place until light or doubled in size, 30 to 60 minutes. Sprinkle with remaining sugar mixture.

Bake at 375° F. for 20 to 30 minutes. Frost with one of the icings on page 102 and decorate with nuts and cherries as desired.

*Christmas Tree:* Line a large cookie sheet with foil; grease. About 3 inches from bottom make a row of 5 cinnamon rolls, overlapping each about ¼ inch. Make next row with 4 rolls, again overlapping onto each other. Continue making rows of 3, 2, and 1. Use 1 roll for the trunk.

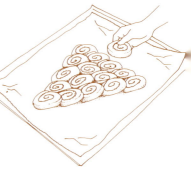

*Cinnamon Rings:* Arrange 8 rolls around the edge of greased 8-inch round pan, overlapping slightly. (Rolls may also be arranged in a heart-shaped pan.)

## Easter Rabbit Coffee Cake

*What fun—a great big Easter Bunny bread. You'll love it with eggs for breakfast.*

**Bake: 350° F. for 25 to 30 minutes       Makes: 1 large Easter rabbit**

- 1 loaf frozen white (sweet or raisin) bread dough, thawed
- 1 tablespoon butter, melted
- 2 tablespoons Cinnamon Sugar, page 103
- Vanilla Icing, page 102
- coconut, if desired
- small gumdrops and colored toothpicks

Let dough rise until almost doubled in size. Cut off one-third of loaf. From remaining two-thirds, cut off two pieces the size of walnuts. Shape larger piece into a 24-inch strip. Coil onto greased cookie sheet, leaving about 3 inches at bottom of sheet. Shape the third of dough into a 15-inch strip. Twist into flat coil and place on cookie sheet so it just touches first coil. Shape small pieces into 4-inch strips; place at top of smaller coil for "ears."

Brush rabbit generously with butter; sprinkle with cinnamon sugar. Cover; let rise in warm place until doubled in size, 30 to 45 minutes.

Bake at 350° F. for 25 to 30 minutes. Cool and frost. Sprinkle with coconut and make a rabbit face with gumdrops and colored toothpicks.

*Snowman:* Divide dough into pieces as described for rabbit. Shape the 2 larger pieces as described for the rabbit. Combine the 2 walnut-size pieces and shape to make a hat. Place on snowman's head. Brush with *butter* and sprinkle with *cinnamon sugar.* Let rise and bake. Add 1 or 2 drops of *blue food coloring* to 1 tablespoon frosting and frost hat. Frost snowman with remaining frosting and sprinkle with *coconut.* Make a snowman face and buttons on body with *gumdrops.* Insert a *sucker* for a broom.

## Cupid's Coffee Cake

*An easy shaping idea results in a heart-shaped cake—no special pans needed.*

**Bake: 350° F. for 25 to 30 minutes     Makes: 2 hearts**

- 1 loaf frozen white (or sweet) bread dough, thawed
- 2 tablespoons butter or margarine, melted
- 1/3 cup sugar
- 1 teaspoon cinnamon
- ¼ cup chopped nuts or coconut, if desired

Let dough rise until doubled in size. Roll out on floured surface to a 20x8-inch rectangle. Brush with butter. Combine sugar, cinnamon and nuts; sprinkle over dough. Roll up, starting with 20-inch side. Seal seam. Cut in half to make two 10-inch pieces. Place one roll on greased cookie sheet. Fold this roll in half; seal ends together. Starting at folded end, cut with scissors down center of roll to within 1 inch of other end. Turn cut halves flat on side, cut-side up, to make heart shape. Repeat with remaining dough. Cover; let rise in warm place until light or doubled in size, 30 to 60 minutes.

Bake at 350° F. for 25 to 30 minutes. If desired, spoon about 2 tablespoons red jelly onto each heart and bake 5 minutes. Frost with Vanilla Icing, page 102.

**Note:** One large heart may be made. Be sure to use a large cookie sheet.

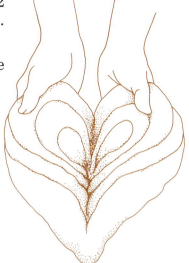

## Easy Danish Kuchen

*An easy coffee cake for the beginner, this fruit-topped coffee cake offers both eye appeal and good eating.*

**Bake: 375° F. for 20 to 25 minutes     Makes: 2 coffee cakes**

- 1 loaf frozen white (or sweet) bread dough, thawed
- 2 tablespoons butter or margarine, melted
- 1 cup prepared fruit pie filling or preserves
- 1 recipe Sugar Streusel, page 103

Let dough rise until doubled in size. Divide in half. Roll out, half at a time, on floured surface to a 12x10-inch rectangle. Brush with half the butter and spread half the filling to within 1 inch of all edges. Fold up about ½ inch of dough on each end. Then fold over about 2 inches on each side, leaving an opening down the center. Place on greased cookie sheets. Sprinkle Sugar Streusel over the tops. Cover; let rise in warm place until light or doubled in size, 30 to 60 minutes.

Bake at 375° F. for 20 to 25 minutes. Frost warm coffee cakes with one of the icings on page 102, if desired.

## Quickie Orange Coffee Cake

*Bubbles of bread are crunchy with orange sugar and gooey on the bottom.*

**Bake: 375° F. for 20 to 25 minutes    Makes: 13x9-inch coffee cake**

- 1 loaf frozen white (or sweet) bread dough, thawed
- ¼ cup butter or margarine, melted
- ¼ cup orange juice
- 1 tablespoon grated orange peel
- 1/3 cup sugar

Cut dough into 36 pieces; place in well-buttered 13x9-inch pan. Combine butter and orange juice; spoon over dough pieces. Mix together peel and sugar; sprinkle over all. Cover; let rise in warm place until very light and more than doubled in size, 1 to 1½ hours.

Bake at 375° F. for 20 to 25 minutes. Immediately loosen edges and turn out on wire rack lined with waxed paper. Best warm.

## Blueberry Flip

*The fruit filling makes this coffee cake a good choice for a breakfast bread.*

**Bake: 375° F. for 20 to 25 minutes     Makes: 2 coffee cakes**

- 1 loaf frozen white (or sweet) bread dough, thawed
- 2 cups fresh or frozen blueberries, thawed
- ¼ cup sugar
- 2 tablespoons flour
- 1 tablespoon butter or margarine

Let dough rise until doubled in size. Combine blueberries, sugar, and flour. Roll out half of dough on floured surface to a 12x10-inch rectangle. Place half of blueberry mixture, lengthwise, down center third of dough. Make diagonal cuts down sides of dough, 3 inches long and 1 inch apart. Alternately fold opposite strips over filling, crossing in center. Seal ends. Place on well-greased cookie sheet. Repeat with remaining dough. Cover; let rise in warm place until light, 30 minutes.

Bake at 375° F. for 20 to 25 minutes. Frost warm coffee cakes with Vanilla Icing, page 102. Or brush with butter and sprinkle with powdered sugar.

*Apple Flip:* The following apple mixture may be used: 3 cups chopped, pared *apples,* ½ cup *raisins,* 1/3 cup *sugar,* 2 tablespoons *flour,* and ½ teaspoon *cinnamon.* Bake at 350° F. for 30 to 35 minutes.

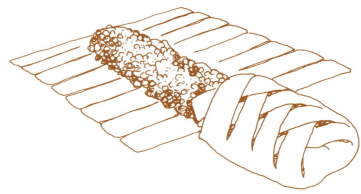

## Butterscotch Coffee Cake

*Butterscotch pudding mix flavors this coffee cake, and it's easy to shape.*

**Bake: 375° F. for 25 to 30 minutes          Makes: 1 coffee cake**

- **1   loaf frozen white (or sweet) bread dough, thawed**
- **¼  cup butter or margarine, melted**
- **1   package butterscotch pudding and pie filling mix (not instant)**
- **½  cup coconut or chopped nuts**

Let dough rise until doubled in size. Roll out on floured surface to a 16x10-inch rectangle. Brush with butter; then sprinkle with pudding mix and coconut. Roll up, starting with 16-inch side. Form into "U" shape; place in greased 9x9- or 10x8-inch pan. With scissors, make cut halfway through center top of the entire "U" shape. Cover; let rise in warm place until light or doubled in size, 30 to 60 minutes.

Bake at 375° F. for 25 to 30 minutes. Remove from pan carefully. Frost warm coffee cake with Vanilla Icing, page 102.

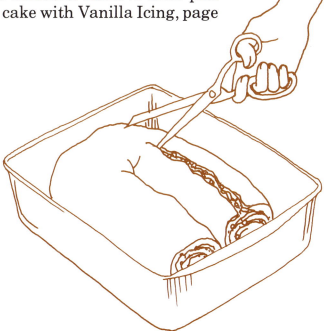

# Ethnic Breads

Bread takes on many shapes, textures, and flavors. Each country in the world has a bread typical of its region, and for this reason we call such breads "ethnic breads." Unleavened bread, the very first bread, is still baked in the Middle East. France and Italy are famous for crusty, light breads while in Northern and Eastern Europe, where rye grain grows, the heavy, sourdough dark breads are popular. Vienna is famous not only for its music, but also for its breads. It was here that "Danish" pastry had its start.

As people come to the United States from many countries, they brought their recipes with them. For many years these recipes stayed in the places where the newcomers made their homes. After World War II, people began moving from one place to another. Today recipes are being shared with people nationwide.

Many recipes for ethnic breads can be adapted to frozen bread dough. This shortcut saves time and makes ethnic breads easy to make, too. Here you'll find many recipes that have been handed down from parent to child through the ages. More ethnic breads can be found in other sections of the book. Check the index for a listing of all the ethnic breads included.

Be sure you have read "Special Know-How for Baking with Frozen Dough," page 11, before you start to bake.

## French Baguettes

*Long, skinny loaves that look like the bread so popular in France. The French way to eat the bread is to have each person break off a chunk. The bread is served with a green salad and cheese after the main course.*

**Bake: 325° F. for 30 to 35 minutes    Makes: 2 (16-inch) loaves**

- 1 loaf frozen white (or French) bread dough, thawed
- 1 tablespoon beaten egg white or egg
- 1 tablespoon water

Let dough rise until almost doubled in size. Divide in half. Shape into 16-inch strips on lightly floured surface. Place on greased cookie sheet. Combine egg and water; brush over loaves. With sharp knife, make several cuts across top of loaf. Cover; let rise in warm place until very light or doubled in size, 45 to 60 minutes.

Bake at 325° F. for 30 to 35 minutes, or until rich golden brown.

## Taos Indian Bread

*This loaf is shaped the way the Pueblo Indians shaped their bread to honor the sun god. Serve it with chili for a Western flair.*

**Bake: 375° F. for 25 to 30 minutes    Makes: 2 loaves**

- 1 loaf frozen white bread dough, thawed

Let dough rise until almost doubled in size. Roll out half of dough to a 10-inch circle. Fold in half; place on greased cookie sheet. Make 6 cuts 2 inches deep, from outside toward fold. Bring folded ends together to make a circle for "sun" and "rays." Cover; let rise in warm place until light or doubled in size, about 1 hour.

Bake at 375° F. for 25 to 30 minutes. Brush hot loaves with butter.

## Golden Braid

*The Swiss, as well as bakers in other countries of Europe, show baking skill by the number of strips of dough they can braid together. The beginner starts with three, and the expert can braid as many as nine strips together.*

**Bake: 375° F. for 25 to 30 minutes    Makes: 1 loaf**

- 1 loaf frozen white (sweet or honey wheat) bread dough, thawed
- 1 tablespoon beaten egg
  sesame seed

Let dough rise until almost doubled in size. Divide into thirds. Shape each into 15-inch strips. Braid together. Pinch ends together. Place on greased cookie sheet. Brush with egg; then sprinkle with sesame seed, if desired. Cover; let rise in warm place until very light, about 1 hour.

Bake at 375° F. for 25 to 30 minutes, or until a rich golden brown.

## Moravian Coffee Cake

*The Pennsylvania Dutch coffee cake. Each time it bakes, it takes on a different shape.*

**Bake: 350° F. for 25 to 30 minutes    Makes: 2 (9x5-inch) coffee cakes**

- 1 loaf frozen white (or sweet) bread dough, thawed
- ½ cup brown sugar
- 1½ teaspoons cinnamon
- ¼ cup chopped nuts
- 6 tablespoons butter or margarine, melted

Let dough rise slightly. Divide in half; press each half into a well-greased 9x5-inch pan. Combine brown sugar, cinnamon, and nuts; sprinkle over dough. Drizzle with butter. Cover; let rise in warm place until doubled in size, 1½ to 2 hours.

Bake at 350° F. for 25 to 30 minutes. Let stand a minute or two; carefully remove from pans onto wire rack lined with waxed paper.

## Hot Cross Buns

*One story says this English bun was first made to honor the goddess of spring. Now it reminds Christians of Good Friday and is sold in bakeries during the Easter season. You, too, can make these buns for Easter or at any time of the year.*

**Bake: 400° F. for 12 to 15 minutes     Makes: 12 to 16 rolls**

- 1 loaf frozen white (or sweet) bread dough, thawed
- ½ cup currants
- ½ teaspoon cinnamon
- 2 tablespoons chopped candied citron, if desired

Let dough rise slightly. Flatten dough to ¼- to ½-inch thickness. Sprinkle with fruits and cinnamon; press down firmly. Roll up; cut into 12 to 16 pieces. Shape into balls, making sure currants are covered. Place 2 inches apart on greased cookie sheet. Cover; let rise in warm place until light or doubled in size, 1 to 1½ hours.

Bake at 400° F. for 12 to 15 minutes. Make a cross on each bun with frosting. Use half the recipe for Vanilla Icing, page 102.

## Julekake

*A fruit-filled bread found in almost all the Norwegian homes at Christmas. Cardamom is one of the favorite spices of Scandinavian countries. Nutmeg or mace can be substituted.*

**Bake: 350° F. for 25 to 30 minutes    Makes: 2 round loaves**

- 1 loaf frozen white (or sweet) bread dough, thawed
- ½ cup raisins
- ¼ cup cut candied cherries
- ¼ cup chopped almonds, if desired
- ½ teaspoon ground or crushed cardamom
- candied cherries
- almonds

Let dough rise until almost doubled in size. Flatten to ½-inch thickness. Sprinkle with the remaining ingredients; press down firmly. Divide dough in half; shape each into balls. Place in greased round cake pans or on a cookie sheet. Cover; let rise in warm place until light or doubled in size, 1 to 1½ hours.

Bake at 350° F. for 25 to 30 minutes. Frost warm loaves with Vanilla Icing, page 102. Decorate with candied cherries and almonds.

Traditional Shaping: After shaping, make ½-inch horizontal cuts, about ½ inch from cookie sheet, all the way around the loaf. Press down in center of loaf with fist.

## Grecian Feast Bread

*The ethnic bread traditionally served on religious days, especially Christmas and Easter. The 3 small loaves form a triangular shape which represents the Trinity. Bread must be cut at the table. Each person is served a small slice from each loaf.*

**Bake: 375° F. for 30 to 35 minutes      Makes: 1 coffee bread**

- **1 loaf frozen white (or sweet) bread dough, thawed**
- **½ cup currants**
- **Vanilla Icing, page 102**
- **candied cherries**
- **whole blanched almonds**

Let dough rise slightly. Flatten to ½-inch thickness; sprinkle with currants. Fold in half, working currants into dough. Divide into thirds; shape each into a ball. Place ½ inch apart on greased cookie sheet, forming triangular shape. Cover; let rise in warm place until light or doubled in size, 1 to 1½ hours.

Bake at 375° F. for 30 to 35 minutes. Frost and make a flower on top of each loaf, using 3 almonds and 3 cherry pieces for the petals in each flower.

## Stollen

*A holiday bread that had its origin in Germany. Years ago it was a breakfast bread, but today it is served at any time of the day. It is shaped like an oversized Parker House roll and is full of Christmas fruits and almonds.*

**Bake: 350° F. for 25 to 30 minutes    Makes: 1 coffee cake**

- 1 loaf frozen white (or sweet) bread dough, thawed
- 1/3 cup almond slices
- ¼ cup raisins
- ¼ cup mixed candied fruit
- 1 teaspoon grated orange peel
- 1 teaspoon grated lemon peel
- ½ teaspoon butter, melted
- 1 tablespoon soft butter or margarine
  powdered sugar

Let dough rise slightly. Roll out on floured surface to a 14x9-inch rectangle. Sprinkle with almonds, fruit, and peels; press into dough. Brush edge of dough with melted butter. Lift long side and fold over to within ½ inch of edge of other side. Place on greased cookie sheet. Cover; let rise in warm place until light or doubled in size, 1 to 1½ hours.

Bake at 350° F. for 25 to 30 minutes. Brush hot bread with soft butter; sprinkle generously with powdered sugar.

# Supper and Snack Breads

In early times bread was an entire meal. At one time during the Middle Ages, bread was baked hard enough to form the platter that held the rest of the meal, and afterwards the "platter" could be eaten. It wasn't very good! Today bread is part of the meal, and bread dough can be used in quick hot dishes, too. It can be the bottom crust of pizza, the outside wrapping for a baked filling, or the crusty, golden brown top for a casserole.

In this section you'll find supper dishes to make when you are cooking for the family. Others you will want to serve at your next birthday party. Still others are grand to bake and freeze so that you'll have them on hand for a quick snack. Reheat them as you would a frozen TV dinner.

Most of these recipes call for meat and other things that spoil quickly. Make these breads at serving time and refrigerate leftovers. If you want to make them ahead of time, refrigerate or freeze them after baking.

Be sure you have read "Special Know-How for Baking with Frozen Dough," page 11, before you start to bake.

## Pizza

"Pizza" is the Italian word for pie. The first pizzas were made many years ago by the people of Naples, Italy. After World War II, American soldiers brought pizza recipes home with them. Ever since, cooks' minds have run wild with hundreds of variations. The making and shaping of the dough is a specialty of many chefs. They love to show their skill by shaping the dough with their hands and flipping it in the air.

A sure way for us to make pizza crusts is to start with frozen bread dough and stretch and roll it out with a rolling pin. In the recipes that follow, you'll learn how to make pizza three different ways with lots of tasty toppings. Pizza should always be eaten piping hot from the oven. The cheese and tomatoes should be bubbling, and the crust should be a crispy, deep golden brown.

## Pizza

*Season pizza to suit your taste. If you want, use an already prepared mix for the sauce and add your favorite topping. If you don't need both pizzas, one can be frozen and reheated at another time.*

**Bake: 450° F. for 15 to 20 minutes       Makes: 2 (13-inch) pizzas**

- 1 loaf frozen white bread dough, thawed
- ½ cup finely chopped onion
- 1 tablespoon olive or cooking oil
- 1 cup (8 oz.) tomato sauce
- ¾ cup (6 oz.) tomato paste
- 1 clove garlic, mashed and chopped
- ½ teaspoon salt
- 1 teaspoon sugar
- ½ teaspoon oregano
- ¼ teaspoon basil
- pinch of pepper
- 2 cups shredded Mozzarella or pizza cheese
- ¼ cup chopped fresh parsley
- 2 tablespoons Parmesan cheese

Let dough rise until doubled in size. Fry onion lightly in oil. Add next 8 ingredients. Simmer 5 minutes. Roll out half of dough on floured surface to a 13-inch circle. Place in greased pizza pan or on greased cookie sheet.

Brush with oil; sprinkle with ½ cup cheese and top with half the tomato mixture. Sprinkle with a topping if desired, and then top with ½ cup cheese and half of the parsley and Parmesan cheese. Repeat with remaining dough.

Bake immediately at 450° F. for 15 to 20 minutes. Serve hot.

*Pizza Toppings:* Quantities given are for one pizza. You may double the amount for both pizzas, or use a different topping on each pizza.

- ½ cup cooked pork sausage
- ½ cup fresh or canned sliced mushrooms
- 1 cup pepperoni, salami, or other Italian sausages, diced, sliced, or in strips
- ½ cup cooked ground beef
- ½ cup sliced frankfurters or bologna
- ¼ cup crumbled fried bacon
- ½ cup chopped ripe olives
- ½ cup tuna

*Pizza Party:* Let dough thaw and rise. Divide into 6 parts. Press each into bottom of greased 9-inch pie pan. Sprinkle with cheese and spread with tomato sauce, a topping and more cheese. Bake at 450° F. for 15 to 20 minutes. (It's always fun to have sauces and toppings ready and then let each person put a pizza together.)

## Deep Dish Pizza

*Another type of pizza, popular in Italy, is the Sicilian pizza. It has a thicker crust and filling.*

**Bake: 425° F. for 15 to 20 minutes    Makes: 3 (9-inch) pizzas**

- 1 loaf frozen white bread dough, thawed
- 1 to 1½ pounds ground beef or unseasoned pork sausage
- 1 small onion, chopped
- 1 can (4 oz.) mushroom stems and pieces, undrained
- 1 cup (8 oz.) canned or cooked tomatoes
- 1 can (6 oz.) tomato paste
- ½ teaspoon salt
- ½ teaspoon sugar
- ½ teaspoon oregano
- ½ teaspoon basil
- ½ teaspoon marjoram
- ½ teaspoon garlic powder
- 2 tablespoons chopped fresh parsley
- 1 cup shredded Mozzarella or pizza cheese

Let dough rise until doubled in size. Cook meat and onion in skillet until meat loses red color. Drain off fat. Stir in remaining ingredients except cheese. Cover; simmer 15 minutes. Cool to warm.

Divide dough into thirds. Press each piece into bottom and sides of well-greased 9-inch pie pan. Spoon filling into shells; spread to cover bottom. Sprinkle with cheese. Let stand 15 minutes.

Bake at 425° F. for 15 to 20 minutes, or until crust is rich golden brown. Serve hot.

## French Bread Pizza

*This is the latest in the world of pizza. A bubbling hot pizza topping smothers baked French bread.*

**Broil: 5 to 8 minutes    Makes: 8 to 10 servings**

- 1 loaf baked French-like Bread, page 25
- 1 pound pork sausage or ground beef
- 1 small onion, chopped
- ½ teaspoon salt
- 1 cup pizza or spaghetti sauce
- 1 cup shredded Mozzarella or pizza cheese
- Parmesan cheese, if desired

Cook sausage with onion and salt in skillet; drain off fat. Split bread in half lengthwise. Spread each half with ½ cup sauce, spreading to edge. Top with meat mixture and then the cheeses.

Broil until hot and cheese melts, 5 to 8 minutes; watch closely.

Suggestion: Use 1 cup of any of the following instead of meat: chopped wieners, salami, chopped mushrooms, or a combination.

## Sandwiches

The sandwich had its beginning in England in the eighteenth century. The Earl of Sandwich loved to gamble. One day, instead of taking time out to eat, he asked for two pieces of bread with meat in between. He gambled with one hand while he ate his food with the other. Others liked the idea and named the handy new snack after him.

The open-faced sandwich, which has no bread on top, began in Denmark. In the towns and cities there, restaurants selling open-faced sandwiches line the streets. The Danes make their sandwiches with every combination of foods you can imagine. Why don't you check the refrigerator for leftovers and make your own open-faced sandwich? A good start is to spread some peanut butter on a slice of bread and then top it with banana slices and raisins. Next time, instead of bananas, chop up some raw or cooked vegetables and sprinkle them on the peanut butter.

Other sandwich ideas in this section include Lebanese Bread, Pocket Bread, and old favorites like Pigs-in-Blankets and Coney Islands.

## Giant Sloppy Joe Sandwiches

*Two giant-size buns, split and filled with tasty ground beef mixture. Makes a fun birthday party sandwich. Make the bread and filling ahead of time. Refrigerate the meat mixture. To serve, reheat the filling, then split and fill the buns.*

**Bake: 400° F. for 20 to 25 minutes**  **Makes: 2 sandwich loaves**
**8 to 10 servings**

- 1 **loaf frozen white (French or Italian) bread dough, thawed**
- 2 **tablespoons soft butter or margarine**
  **flour**
  **seasoned salt**

Let dough rise slightly. Divide in half. Press out each half to 10x4-inch rectangle. Place on greased cookie sheet. Brush tops generously with butter. Coat generously with flour and sprinkle with seasoned salt. Cover; let rise in warm place until light or doubled in size, 1 to 1½ hours.

Bake at 400° F. for 20 to 25 minutes. To serve, cut loaves in half lengthwise. Butter lightly and fill with Sloppy Joe mixture. Cut each loaf into 4 or 5 servings.

**Sloppy Joe Filling:**
- 1 pound ground beef
- ½ cup chopped onion
- 1 cup catsup
- ¼ cup water
- 2 tablespoons brown sugar
- 1 teaspoon salt
- 1 teaspoon Worcestershire sauce
- ½ teaspoon dry mustard
- ¼ teaspoon pepper

Brown meat and onion together. Stir in remaining ingredients. Cover; simmer or cook slowly 30 minutes.

Tip: For 4 or 5 servings, freeze one of the baked loaves and half the filling for another time.

## Lebanese Bread

*Another ethnic bread. These round, crusty loaves are about an inch high when baked. They are fun to serve with a dinner, or make them American with your favorite sandwich filling.*

**Bake: 400° F. for 15 to 20 minutes     Makes: 3 round flat loaves**

**1  loaf frozen white (honey wheat or French) bread dough, thawed
    soft butter or margarine**

Let dough rise until doubled in size. Divide into thirds. Roll out each to an 8-inch circle (¼ inch thick) on floured surface. Place on greased cookie sheets. Cover; let rise in warm place until doubled in size, 30 to 60 minutes.

Bake at 400° F. for 15 to 20 minutes. Brush hot loaves with butter.

**Sandwich Ideas:**

Slice Lebanese bread in half crosswise to make 2 thin slices and fill. For a warm sandwich wrap in foil and heat in

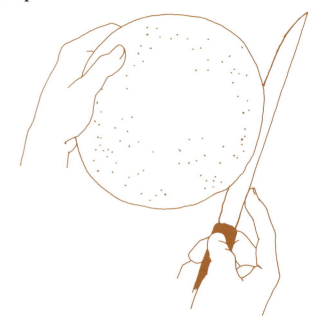

350° F. oven about 15 minutes. To serve, cut into quarters. Use any of these fillings:

* Corned beef, well-drained sauerkraut, Swiss cheese
* Boiled ham, cheese, lettuce
* Bacon, lettuce, tomatoes
* Sloppy Joe ground beef filling, page 93
* Taco filling—chopped tomato, lettuce, and shredded cheese
* Poor boy filling—luncheon meats, cheeses, pickles, onion, lettuce
* Hot broiled frankfurters, sliced, and hot pork and beans

## Pigs-in-Blankets

*A fun supper idea—hot dogs wrapped in a blanket of bread.*

**Bake: 375° F. for 15 to 20 minutes       Makes: 16 (8 servings)**

- 1 loaf frozen white (honey wheat or French) bread dough, thawed
- 16 frankfurters or precooked sausages
     mustard, pickle relish, or catsup, if desired

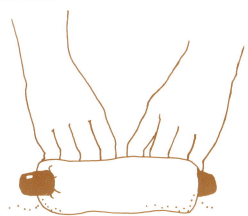

Let dough rise until doubled in size. Divide into 16 pieces. Flatten each to a 4-inch square on floured surface. Place a little mustard or other seasoning sauce in center. Top with frankfurter; bring dough around and seal well. Place, seam-side down, on greased cookie sheet. Cover; let rise in warm place 30 minutes.

Bake at 375° F. for 15 to 20 minutes. Serve warm.

## Coney Islands

*These grilled frankfurters, topped with hot baked beans, are an old favorite. Open the can of beans and heat on the grill.*

**Bake: 400° F. for 15 to 20 minutes   Makes: 6 or 8 servings**

- 1 loaf frozen white (or honey wheat) bread dough, thawed
- 1 can (15 oz.) baked beans
- 6 or 8 frankfurters
  seasoned salt

Divide dough into 6 or 8 pieces. Shape each into oblong bun about 5 inches long. Place on greased cookie sheet. Sprinkle with seasoned salt. Cover; let rise in warm place until light or doubled in size, 1 to 1½ hours.

Bake at 400° F. for 15 to 20 minutes. To serve, split each bun and fill with a grilled frankfurter and hot baked beans.

## Super Sandwiches

*A good way to use small amounts of leftover meats. Make them for a family picnic.*

**Bake: 400° F. for 12 to 15 minutes   Makes: 12 sandwiches**

- 1 loaf frozen (any flavor except sweet) bread dough, thawed
  soft butter
  meats and cheeses (see below)
  mustard, barbecue sauce, catsup, as desired

Let dough rise until doubled in size. Divide into 12 pieces. Flatten to 5-inch circle. Dot center with a small amount of butter. Place a generous amount of 3x2-inch pieces of meat and/or cheese on each. Dot with mustard or a seasoning sauce. Moisten edges with water; fold in half and seal well. Snip top with scissors. (Whenever a filling bakes inside bread or pastry, it is necessary to prick or slit the top for the escape of steam. The edges must be well sealed to prevent the juices from running out. To seal, moisten inside edges and press down firmly with floured fork or fingers.) Place on greased cookie sheet. Cover; let rise in warm place 30 minutes.

Bake at 400° F. for 12 to 15 minutes. Serve warm or cold. Do not keep unrefrigerated for a long period of time.

### Meats and Cheeses:

*Ham Sandwiches:* Slices or cubes of baked or boiled *ham* and *mustard* or well-drained *pickle relish*.

*Ham and Cheese Sandwiches: Ham* as above and *Swiss* or *pizza cheese. Cheddar cheese* can be used too, but be sure to seal well.

*Corned Beef Sandwiches:* Use slices or cubes of *corned beef* with *Swiss* or other *cheese* and a small spoonful of well-drained *sauerkraut*. Season with one or more of the following: *mustard, horseradish sauce, caraway seed* or *mayonnaise*.

*Salami Sandwiches:* Use any kind of cold cut *meats* cut in small pieces and stacked; season as desired. Add slices of *cheese* or *pickles*, if desired.

*Chopped Beef Sandwiches:* Thin-sliced chopped *pressed beef, ham,* or *corned beef* makes good sandwiches. Use it alone or in combination with *cheese* and seasonings.

*Turkey or Chicken Sandwiches:* Slices of cooked *turkey* or *chicken* seasoned with *salt* and *pepper*, plain, or in combination with *Swiss* or *pizza cheese*.

*Tuna-Cheese Sandwiches:* Use *tuna* alone or in combination with a *cheese*.

(These are just a few filling combinations that can go into Super Sandwiches. Sandwiches can be baked and frozen and then be ready to take on a picnic or a boating, camping, or fishing trip. Take frozen; they'll thaw on the way.)

## Barbecue Beef Loaf

*A barbecue beef mixture full of cheese bakes atop a split loaf of French bread. A good supper after water skiing or a ballgame. Make the filling beforehand and bake after you come home.*

**Bake: 375° F. for 30 to 35 minutes     Makes: 6 to 8 servings**

- 1 baked loaf French-like Bread, page 25
- 1 pound lean ground beef
- 1 cup (8-oz. can) tomato sauce
- 1/3 cup chopped onion
- 1 cup shredded Cheddar or American cheese
- ½ teaspoon each: sugar, salt, and chili powder

Split bread in half lengthwise. Combine remaining ingredients. Spread meat mixture over bread halves. Place on cookie sheet.

Bake open-faced at 375° F. for 30 to 35 minutes, or until meat is done.

Note: If you make the filling early, refrigerate it. Put it on the bread just before you bake it.

## Beef Pasties

*Adapted from the pasty that was lunch for miners in Cornwall, England. These same pasties have been a popular food in the iron-mining areas of Minnesota and the Upper Peninsula of Michigan. The original was baked inside a pastry crust. The bread covering makes these pasties taste much like a beef sandwich.*

**Bake: 375° F. for 15 to 20 minutes     Makes: 6 large pasties**

- 1 loaf frozen white bread dough, thawed
- 1 pound lean ground beef (1½ pounds regular)
- 1 medium potato, pared and chopped
- 1 carrot, pared and chopped
- 1 medium onion, chopped
- 1 stalk celery, chopped
- 1 teaspoon salt
- ⅛ teaspoon pepper
- 1 teaspoon mixed herbs (thyme, oregano, marjoram, parsley)

Let dough rise until doubled in size. Combine remaining ingredients in large skillet; cook 20 minutes. Cool to lukewarm. Divide dough into 6 pieces; roll out and stretch each on floured surface to 8-inch circle. Top each with about 2/3 cup filling. Moisten edges; fold in half and seal well with floured fork. With scissors, snip a short gash on top of each. Place on greased cookie sheet. Cover; let rise in warm place 30 minutes.

Bake at 375° F. for 15 to 20 minutes. Serve warm. (Can be served cold, but keep refrigerated until serving time.)

Note: For medium-sized pasties, divide dough into 12 pieces and roll each to a 6-inch circle and top with 1/3 cup filling.

## Miniature Dinner Rolls

*Tiny rolls to fill with tiny squares of meat and cheese—fine for a quick snack.*

**Bake: 400° F. for 10 to 12 minutes    Makes: 36 small rolls**

- 1 loaf frozen white (or honey wheat) bread dough, thawed

Let dough rise slightly. Divide into thirds; then divide each third into 12 pieces. Shape into balls; place on greased cookie sheet. Cover; let rise in warm place until light or doubled in size, 45 to 60 minutes.

Bake at 400° F. for 10 to 12 minutes.

## Mini-Barbecue Hamburgers

*Split the miniature dinner rolls, above, and fill with the hamburger—good for a slumber party.*

**Simmer: 45 minutes    Makes: 36 small meatballs**

- 1½ pounds ground beef
- 1/3 cup finely chopped onion
- ¼ cup bread crumbs
- 2 tablespoons milk
- 1 teaspoon salt
- ⅛ teaspoon pepper

Combine all ingredients; mix thoroughly. Shape into 1-inch balls; then flatten to ½ inch to make little hamburgers. (Keep hands moist for easy shaping.) Brown in hot greased skillet. Drain off fat. Pour Barbecue Sauce over the hamburgers. Cover and simmer or bake in 350° F. oven 45 minutes.

*Barbecue Sauce:* Combine ¼ cup chopped *onion*, 1 cup *catsup*, 1 tablespoon *brown sugar*, 1 tablespoon *lemon juice*, 1 teaspoon *salt*, 1 teaspoon *Worcestershire sauce*, a pinch of *pepper*, a pinch of *cloves*, and a drop of *smoke sauce*. Pour over hamburgers.

## Pocket Bread

*It's fun to make your own pocket bread. This old Middle Eastern bread has suddenly become very popular. The flat circles of dough puff during baking, leaving a hole (pocket) in the middle. Split the side and fill the pocket for a great sandwich.*

**Bake: 425° F. for 8 to 10 minutes   Makes: 10**

**1 loaf frozen white or whole wheat dough, thawed
soft or melted butter (about 2 teaspoons)**

Let dough rise until doubled in size. Divide into 10 equal pieces; then divide each piece in half. Flatten a piece of dough to about 3 inches on a heavily floured surface. Brush center to about ½ inch of the edge with butter. Flatten a second piece of dough to 3 inches. Place on top of the first. Roll out with rolling pin to about 6 inches. Be sure the dough rounds are well dusted with flour. Sprinkle a greased cookie sheet with cornmeal. Place round on cookie sheet. Cover; let rest no more than 15 to 20 minutes.

Bake at 425° F. for 8 to 10 minutes. To serve, split the side and fill pocket with chopped, cooked meats; cheeses; vegetables; or as desired. Serve warm or cold.

# Special Recipes

It takes only a small amount of icing for coffee cakes and rolls. Use just enough to add a sweet touch. Place the rest in a small container and refrigerate. Use it the next time you bake. When icing warm bread, the icing should be stiff or hold its shape when spread. The warmth of the bread will melt the icing so it will spread. If the bread is cold, the icing should be soft enough so it can be spread thinly and will run down the sides of the bread.

## ICINGS

### Vanilla or Almond Icing

- 1 cup powdered sugar
- 1 tablespoon soft butter or margarine
- ½ teaspoon vanilla or almond extract
- 3 to 4 teaspoons milk

Combine all ingredients, mixing until smooth. For frosting warm breads, add milk until icing is thin enough to spread. If breads are frosted cold, you will want to add more milk to get an icing that will run slightly down the sides.

*Orange Icing:* Use *orange juice* instead of milk and add 2 teaspoons *grated orange peel.*

*Lemon Icing:* Use *lemon juice* instead of milk and add 1 teaspoon *grated lemon peel.*

## Egg Wash

*This is what bakers use to give bread a shiny crust. It is also used to hold sesame, poppy, and other seeds to the crust. The usual proportions are equal amounts of slightly beaten egg or egg white and water or milk. A little of the mixture goes a long way.*

- 1 tablespoon slightly beaten egg or egg white
- 1 tablespoon water or milk

Combine the egg and water. Brush carefully over bread as directed in recipe. (For a shinier and crisper crust decrease water to 1 teaspoon.) Egg wash may be brushed on the dough after shaping. Some people like to brush the breads after they have risen. This must be done carefully with a soft brush so the risen dough will not collapse.

## Flavored Sugars

*Flavored sugars are good to sprinkle on hot buttered toast for an after-school snack.*

*Cinnamon Sugar:* Combine ½ cup *sugar* and 2 teaspoons *cinnamon*.

*Sugar Streusel:* Mix together ½ cup *flour*, 2 tablespoons *sugar*, and ¼ teaspoon *nutmeg* or *cinnamon*. Cut 2 tablespoons *butter* or *margarine* into the mixture with a fork until it makes fine crumbs. (This topping is used for a number of coffee cakes and rolls in this book.)

# Index

**Bread Loaves**

An Old-Fashioned Loaf .......... 22
Bubble Dinner Bread ............ 29
Butter Crust Vienna Bread ...... 19
Checkered Loaf ................. 30
Cheese Bubble Loaf ............. 26
Cheese Swirl ................... 31
Cinnamon Swirl Bread ........... 31
French Baguettes ............... 80
French-like Bread .............. 25
Golden Braid ................... 81
Golden Crown ................... 27
Grilled Cheese Sandwich ........ 20
Half n' Half Bread ............. 30
Hearth Bread ................... 18
Honey Bee Twist ................ 28
Individual Loaves .............. 24
Lebanese Bread ................. 94
Mix and Match Bread ............ 30
Oatmeal Wheat Bread ............ 20
Pan Bread ...................... 20
Peanut Butter Swirl ............ 31
Raisin Bread ................... 26
Step-by-Step Method ............ 22
Taos Indian Bread .............. 80
Triple Treat Loaf .............. 28
Two-Tone Swirl ................. 30
White Mountain Loaf ............ 19

**Dinner Rolls**

Butter Crumb Rolls ............. 44
Butter-Crust Rolls ............. 40
Cloverleaf Rolls ............... 38
Crescents ...................... 39
Dinner Buns .................... 37
Dinner Rolls ............... 35, 37
Double-Quick Dinner Rolls ...... 40
Finger Rolls ................... 38
Frankfurter Buns ............... 41
Hamburger Buns ................. 41
Hamburger Hearth Buns .......... 42
Hero Buns ...................... 43
Honey Rolls .................... 44
Hot Cross Buns ................. 83

Miniature Dinner Rolls ......... 100
Oatmeal Hamburger Wheat Buns  42
Oatmeal Wheat Rolls ........... 42
Pan Rolls ..................... 37
Peanut Butter Secrets.......... 45
Pocket Bread ................. 101
Super Hamburger Buns.......... 41
Step-by-Step Method ........... 35
White Mountain Rolls .......... 39

**Sweet Rolls**

Butterscotch Nut Buns ......... 52
Caramel Nut Rolls ............. 53
Cinnamon Buns................. 52
Danish Butter Crispies ......... 54
Danish Rolls .................. 55
Danish "S" Rolls .............. 55
Elephant Ears................. 54
Grandma's Raisin Sugar Rolls ... 56
Hot Cross Buns ................ 83
Jelly Rolls ................... 57
Marshmallow Nuggets........... 59
Mom's Cinnamon Rolls ...... 49, 51
Orange Buns .................. 52
Orange Sticky Rolls ........... 58
Peanut au Chocolat Secrets ..... 45
Peanut Butter Jelly Rolls ....... 57
Ranch-Style Cinnamon Rolls .... 60
Step-by-Step Method ........... 49

**Coffee Breads and Cakes**

Apple Flip .................... 76
Apple Kuchen ................. 66
Blueberry Flip................. 76
Butterscotch Bubble Loaf ....... 67
Butterscotch Coffee Cake ....... 77
Christmas Tree................ 70
Cinnamon Rings ............... 70
Cinnamon Roll Coffee Cake .... 70
Cupid's Coffee Cake ........... 73
Dutch Sugar Cake ............. 65
Easy Danish Kuchen ........... 74
Easter Rabbit Coffee Cake ...... 71
Frosty Snowball Cakes ......... 68
Grecian Feast Bread............ 85
Honey Bee Twist .............. 28
Julekake ..................... 84
Monkey Bread................. 66
Moravian Coffee Cake .......... 82
Quickie Orange Coffee Cake .... 75
Snowman ..................... 72
Step-by-Step Method ........... 63
Stollen ....................... 86
Streusel Coffee Cake ........ 63, 65
Swedish Cinnamon Coffee Cake . 65
Swedish Tea Ring .............. 68

**Ethnic Breads**

Apple Kuchen ................. 66

Beef Pasties . . . . . . . . . . . . . . . . . . . . 99
Deep Dish Pizza . . . . . . . . . . . . . . . . 90
French Baguettes . . . . . . . . . . . . . . . 80
French Bread Pizza . . . . . . . . . . . . . 91
Golden Braid . . . . . . . . . . . . . . . . . . 81
Grecian Feast Bread . . . . . . . . . . . . 85
Hot Cross Buns . . . . . . . . . . . . . . . . 83
Julekake . . . . . . . . . . . . . . . . . . . . . . 84
Lebanese Bread . . . . . . . . . . . . . . . . 94
Moravian Coffee Cake . . . . . . . . . . 82
Pizza . . . . . . . . . . . . . . . . . . . . . . . . . 88
Pocket Bread . . . . . . . . . . . . . . . . . 101
Stollen . . . . . . . . . . . . . . . . . . . . . . . 86
Streusel Coffee Cake . . . . . . . . . 63, 65
Swedish Tea Ring . . . . . . . . . . . . . . 68
Taos Indian Bread . . . . . . . . . . . . . 80

**Supper and Snack Breads**

Barbecue Beef Loaf . . . . . . . . . . . . . 98
Barbecue Sauce . . . . . . . . . . . . . . . 101
Beef Pasties . . . . . . . . . . . . . . . . . . . 99
Bubble Dinner Bread . . . . . . . . . . . 29
Cheese Bubble Loaf . . . . . . . . . . . . 26
Chicken Sandwiches . . . . . . . . . . . . 97
Chopped Beef Sandwiches . . . . . . . 97
Coney Islands . . . . . . . . . . . . . . . . . 96
Corned Beef Sandwiches . . . . . . . . 97

Deep Dish Pizza . . . . . . . . . . . . . . . 90
French Bread Pizza . . . . . . . . . . . . 91
Giant Sloppy Joe Sandwiches . . . . 92
Grilled Cheese Sandwich . . . . . . . . 20
Ham and Cheese Sandwiches . . . . 97
Ham Sandwiches . . . . . . . . . . . . . . . 97
Lebanese Bread . . . . . . . . . . . . . . . . 94
Mini-Barbecue Hamburgers . . . . . 100
Miniature Dinner Rolls . . . . . . . . . 100
Pigs-in-Blankets . . . . . . . . . . . . . . . . 95
Pizza . . . . . . . . . . . . . . . . . . . . . . . . . 88
Pizza Toppings . . . . . . . . . . . . . . . . 89
Pocket Bread . . . . . . . . . . . . . . . . . 101
Salami Sandwiches . . . . . . . . . . . . . 97
Sandwich Ideas . . . . . . . . . . . . . . . . 94
Super Sandwiches . . . . . . . . . . . . . . 96
Tuna-Cheese Sandwiches . . . . . . . . 98
Turkey Sandwiches . . . . . . . . . . . . . 97

**Special Recipes**

Almond Icing . . . . . . . . . . . . . . . . 102
Cinnamon Sugar . . . . . . . . . . . . . . 103
Egg Wash . . . . . . . . . . . . . . . . . . . . 103
Lemon Icing . . . . . . . . . . . . . . . . . 103
Orange Icing . . . . . . . . . . . . . . . . . 102
Sugar Streusel . . . . . . . . . . . . . . . . 103
Vanilla Icing . . . . . . . . . . . . . . . . . 102

## About the Author

Sylvia Ogren is recognized nationwide as an outstanding authority on bread baking and, as a former elementary schoolteacher, she has a special interest in children and their first baking experiences. A home economics consultant, she has worked for many major food companies, including the Pillsbury Company, where she supervised much of the work behind the Pillsbury Bake-Off Contest.

Ms. Ogren earned a Bachelor's and a Master's degree in Home Economics at the University of Minnesota. She has written newspaper columns, developed thousands of recipes for cookbooks and recipe leaflets, supervised publication of the Pillsbury Bake-Off cookbooks, and helped to compile the original *Pillsbury Family Cookbook*. She has also developed cookbooks for the Peavy Company (Occident/King Midas Flour), including the well-known Bar Cookie cookbooks.

## About the Illustrator

Christine Wold Dyrud is a free-lance artist specializing in children's books.

**OTHER**

**PAPER BY KIDS** by Arnold E. Grummer

**IT'S NOT REALLY MAGIC** by Rosella J. Schroeder and Marie C. Sanderson
*Microwave Cooking for Young People*

Both *Shape It and Bake It* and *Bake Breads From Frozen Dough,* the comprehensive adult cookbook on which this children's version is based, are available at your favorite bookstore. Or they may be ordered direct from the publisher. The price of the adult book, a spiral-bound paperback, is $6.95, and the price of the children's book is $7.95. Please add $.75 for postage and handling.

Send your check or money order to

Dillon Press, Inc.
500 South Third Street
Minneapolis, MN 55415